ROUTLEDGE LIBRARY EDITIONS:
TRADE UNIONS

I0127921

Volume 14

ECONOMIC EXPANSION AND STRUCTURAL CHANGE

ECONOMIC EXPANSION AND STRUCTURAL CHANGE

A Trade Union Manifesto

Edited and Translated by
T. L. JOHNSTON

Routledge
Taylor & Francis Group
LONDON AND NEW YORK

First published in 1963 by George Allen & Unwin Ltd.

This edition first published in 2023
by Routledge
4 Park Square, Milton Park, Abingdon, Oxon OX14 4RN

and by Routledge
605 Third Avenue, New York, NY 10158

Routledge is an imprint of the Taylor & Francis Group, an informa business

British Library Cataloguing in Publication Data
A catalogue record for this book is available from the British Library

ISBN: 978-1-032-37553-3 (Set)
ISBN: 978-1-032-39415-2 (Volume 14) (hbk)
ISBN: 978-1-032-39421-3 (Volume 14) (pbk)
ISBN: 978-1-003-34961-7 (Volume 14) (ebk)

DOI: 10.4324/9781003349617

Publisher's Note
The publisher has gone to great lengths to ensure the quality of this reprint but points out that some imperfections in the original copies may be apparent.

Disclaimer
The publisher has made every effort to trace copyright holders and would welcome correspondence from those they have been unable to trace.

ECONOMIC EXPANSION
AND
STRUCTURAL CHANGE

A TRADE UNION MANIFESTO

Report submitted to the 16th Congress of
LANDSORGANISATIONEN I SVERIGE
(*The Swedish Confederation of Trade Unions*)

EDITED AND TRANSLATED BY
T. L. JOHNSTON
Author of *Collective Bargaining in Sweden*

London
GEORGE ALLEN & UNWIN LTD
RUSKIN HOUSE MUSEUM STREET

Translated from the Swedish

PRINTED IN GREAT BRITAIN
in 10 *on* 11 *pt Times Roman type*
BY SIMSON SHAND LTD
LONDON, HERTFORD AND HARLOW

CONTENTS

CONTENTS

CONTENTS

Contents

INTRODUCTION

The Swedish Confederation of Trade Unions—*Landsorganisationen*, or LO, as it is habitually called—enjoys an international reputation as a model trade union movement, with a clear system of government and exhilarating policy ideas about the major problems of collective bargaining. By international standards it is a small trade union movement, with 1·5 million members organized in forty-one unions, of which the largest is the Metal Workers' Union with 300,000 members. LO can now claim that about one Swede in five is affiliated to an LO union. The unions organize on the industrial principle, and cover practically the whole labour market as regards manual workers. LO also organizes a significant number of salaried employees, though it is not the main central body for non-manual trade unionists in Sweden.

In the past twenty-five years the organized groups that are active in the Swedish labour market have shown a great willingness to evolve codes of conduct for labour relations. LO and the Swedish Employers' Confederation—S.A.F.—have concluded a number of central agreements on the most vexed questions of industrial relations, and from its side LO has reformed its internal government so that such problems as demarcation disputes are almost unknown while collective bargaining procedures have been altered to provide a strong central focus for co-ordinating the unions' wage bargaining demands.

The report which is translated here brings together in a systematic exposition the fruits of recent trade union thinking in Sweden on the problems of economic growth and the structural changes inevitably associated with it. It is the work of a group of LO economists—Dr Rudolf Meidner, who acted as chairman, Tord Ekström, Clas-Erik Odhner, Eric Pettersson, Lillemor Erlander, all of whom are members of the LO research division,—plus Dr Kurt Samuelsson. The study was prepared for, and debated at, the quinquennial LO congress in the autumn of 1961, and it has already been the subject of lively debate and discussion in Sweden.

The presentation of a general theme for consideration is indeed becoming an established tradition at LO congresses. In 1941 LO produced the first of its major studies, *The Trade Union Movement and Industry*, in which the problems of trade unionism were analysed in the context of the whole economy and community. The LO congress of that year was a landmark in the reform of the government of the unions to take account of wider social and economic objectives

11

than are traditionally associated with a trade union movement, and the study set a precedent which has happily been followed.

The 1941 document was not translated, but in 1951 the international reader was able to sample the quality of LO thinking on problems of applied economics in the LO Report on *Trade Unions and Full Employment*, which impressed by its sweep and sophisticated discussion of economic stabilization and wage policy.

The present study continues this established tradition of constructive thinking and broad perspective. In retrospect, it can be seen to have evolved out of the 1941 report, which emphasized the positive role the unions must play in the community and stressed the importance of rationalization as the essential foundation of progressive unionism, and of the 1951 document, with its lucid treatment of stabilization, structural change, and labour market policy.

More recently, the pressure of urgent structural economic problems in such sectors as textiles and agriculture has provided an additional impulse, which has led to a great deal of empirical work on structural problems and to the study of policies for appropriate changes in the structure of the economy. The report has thus built on previous systematic thinking and also on recent experience. In the latter sense, an additional source for the report is to be found in the stimulus provided by an articulate and responsive trade union membership. The Textile Workers' Union, for example, has been severely hit by the contraction of the industry, but its response has not be restrictionist. It has recognized the need for the kind of adaptability which is such a central strand running through the pages which follow.

The international reader is asked to remember that this document wears the badges of its origins. As a study submitted to a trade union congress for debate and deliberation, it is challenging and radical in its strain. The authors deliberately attempted to provide a stimulus by boldly stating their particular view of problems and policies, and the translated version endeavours to retain this distinctive flavour.

The authors are, for example, trenchant in their criticisms of recent credit policy in Sweden; eloquent in their plea for free trade, and scornful of a protectionist outlook; controversial on company taxation, wage policy, and the proposal that Branch Rationalization Funds should be set up for particular industries through the machinery of collective bargaining; invigorating in their discussion of labour market and location policy; reassuring in their emphasis on growth and change. Here is the stuff of controversy.

Above all, the study shows a real sense of urgency in espousing the cause of international solidarity, and interpreting this as a moral and economic obligation to provide aid to the under-developed countries.

This alone makes this document an important contribution to contemporary social and economic thinking on economic development, and provides adequate justification for making it available to a wider circle of readers than those familiar with the Swedish language.

The prudent translator who is anxious to protect himself from the zealous detective work of bi-lingual readers does well to provide himself with a safeguard: accordingly, this is more a transplanting than a translation. There has been some minor editing, but every effort has been made to retain the emphasis and flavour of the original Swedish text. It is the hope of the authors and the translator that the anglicized version will thrive in this alien soil, and that the international public will be able to catch some of the contagion and the challenge of current Swedish trade union thinking on this vital theme.

T.L.J.

PART I

THE GENERAL FRAMEWORK

CHAPTER I

THE RISE OF INDUSTRY

Sweden is one of the rich industrially developed countries of the world. To attain this position, with its industrial capacity and wide production possibilities, she has had to undergo a continuous process of transformation and change in the structure of her economy, in the conditions of work, and in the life of her society.

For human beings the changes have often involved a great sacrifice of individual happiness and liberty. During the initial stages of industrialization in the old 'liberal' society it was largely the pressure of need and compulsion which drove people to the new types of activity, not hope, expectation, and the attraction of a new and better way of life. Nevertheless the new industrial era, despite its insecurity and starvation wages, came as a salvation to the agrarian society of the mid-nineteenth century. The pressure of population had produced unemployment and the most miserable degradation, and the first major structural changes of industrialization thus occurred in an economy whose foundations had gradually been crumbling. This explains much of the social discontent with which the industrialization process was long associated, although it is also true that the early liberal industrial society did itself tolerate conditions of work, a social environment, and economic and social pressures on human beings which were unnecessarily harsh and immiserating.

As the amount of capital grew and productivity increased, and as the workers' trade union and political organizations became more influential, protective legislation and social policy reforms were enacted which mitigated the worst hardships. Thereafter it proved possible to reconcile the continuous changes in the economy more successfully with greater security and freedom for the masses, and with a higher yield from the expanding resources of production in the form of an increase in welfare for large groups of the population. However, there still remained the scourge of lengthy crises and depressions to interrupt progress—a severe and costly 'method' of bringing pressure to bear for the purpose of eliminating inefficient enterprises and forcing capital and labour to shift to more expanding sectors. In this way the insistence that expansion and structural change should be combined with full employment came to form one of the corner-stones of the ideology of the trade union and political working class movement.

B   17

This is not the place to attempt to give a detailed account of the way in which the major structural changes, from the beginnings of industrialization to our modern welfare state, have proceeded, with their economic, social, political and technical impulses and ramifications. Let us simply recall some of the main features.

Industrialization in Sweden was impelled from abroad. The growth of industry involved greater specialization, and this could never have been carried so far if in the first instance it had been a purely national phenomenon. Sweden was far too small a country to be able to achieve successful specialization within her own boundaries, for in many cases this necessitates large-scale mass production if it is to be profitable, and mass production in turn requires large markets.

A small country must specialize in relation to other countries if its advantages are to be obtained to the full. If in addition there are, as in Sweden, large resources of raw materials which cannot be fully utilized within the country the need for foreign markets becomes much greater. Industrialization abroad, therefore, first in the United Kingdom and in Belgium, and later in France and in Germany, was the main driving force behind Swedish industrialization. The demand for our most important raw materials, iron ore and timber, made the iron ore industry and forestry increasingly profitable and led to larger and more mechanized productions units. Together with the development of railways and other means of communications, this provided the basis for a domestic engineering industry, which operated initially as the service and repair handmaid of the iron ore mills and the forest industries, but soon became a manufacturing industry, producing machines and gradually exporting semi-finished and finished products. By about the year 1870 the preparatory period for industrialization had come to an end and the real take-off and increasingly rapid transformation to an industrial country could follow. The speed at which this took place can be discerned from some simple population statistics. Of a population of just over 4 million in the year 1870, over 70 per cent was employed in agriculture and subsidiary occupations, only 15 per cent in industry and handicrafts, and 5 per cent in commerce and communications. Forty years later, of a population of $5\frac{1}{2}$ million—that after an emigration in the period 1860–1910 of almost precisely one million persons—not quite 50 per cent was occupied in agriculture and related occupations, over 30 per cent in industry and handicrafts, and nearly 15 per cent in commerce and communications. The urban population had grown from 15 per cent to 40 per cent.

By then industrialization had assumed the basic form and features which it still to a large extent retains. Different branches of the economy have subsequently developed to very different degrees, and

18

commerce, transport and service occupations in particular have grown much more rapidly than manufacturing industry proper. In the year 1955, 25 per cent of the working population was engaged in commerce and service occupations and 33 per cent in industry and handicrafts. The major raw material industries have gradually become processing industries as well, and the continuance of mechanization in agriculture has made possible a further major movement of workers to the growing urban industries, so that agriculture and ancillary occupations now account for only about 15 per cent. The urban population is now larger than the rural population. But the 'heavy' sectors of industry are still broadly the same: forest and ore enterprises, and those 'Swedish genius' industries established about the turn of the century to exploit Swedish inventions through firms which became internationally renowned in ball-bearings, the electro-technical and telephone industry, the separator industry, the manufacture of turbines, and so on.

A richly differentiated domestic consumer goods industry also grew up, partly through the protection which became increasingly strong after 1900, and also of course by virtue of the increase in demand which resulted from the growth of towns, rising incomes, and the increasing need to purchase goods instead of making them at home. The manufacture of textiles had well-established traditions. The manufacture of shoes, building materials, foodstuffs and luxuries were newer, and some of the food stuffs industries such as flour mills, bakeries, margarine and sugar factories began to develop more rapidly only about the year 1900. The First World War cut off much foreign competition and, after the temporary revival of commerce in the 1920s, the protectionist tendencies of the 1930s and the new restrictions of the Second World War and its aftermath made it easier to continue to develop consumer goods enterprises, although not always in rational forms.

It is often argued that the main characteristics of the early years of industrialization were severe competition between different firms, the dispersion of power, and 'atomism'. This is very largely erroneous. On the contrary, the 'liberal society' was marked by far-reaching concentration of power and influence in the hands of a relatively small set of officials, businessmen, owners of capital and politicians. A small group at the top in fact had a monopoly of everything, the structure of the economy, political influence, culture, learning, and ownership. Free competition in economic matters existed on paper, but in reality it was severely curtailed. In those sectors of enterprise which pioneered the movement towards greater industrialization explicit monopoly was more or less the essential feature. Inertia in techniques and high fixed costs gave almost every new industrial entrepreneur an advantage which he could often hold for a considerable period. Likewise, transport conditions often reduced the power of foreign competition and sometimes gave domestic firms a sort of geographical monopoly. With the passage of time mergers took place and cartels were formed, and the credit system, which was reasonably well organized by 1900 and subsequently became increasingly concentrated in the hands of a few large banks, served to strengthen these tendencies. The crises of the inter-war years and technical and market changes during and after the Second World War intensified the movement towards the formation of cartels, mergers, and vertical and horizontal integration. A rich flora of small-scale enterprises has at the same time been able to flourish under the patronage of the large firms and concerns, as distributors, as sub-contractors to the large firms, or in a sort of 'free' sector, sometimes protected by the rigid pricing of the large enterprises.

This concentration has by no means only had disadvantages. In retrospect, its major benefit has been quicker and more rational industrialization than would otherwise have been possible. The technical and cost advantages of large-scale production are perfectly obvious *per se*. The strong position occupied by these enterprises has frequently created a sort of 'power of taxation', the possibilities of retaining and ploughing back profits and financing rapid expansion, which has stimulated growth. The main disadvantage has been the great accumulation of property by a small number of persons and the accompanying concentration of power in their hands. This could be particularly harmful as long as the important countervailing influences of the state, the trade union movement, and the consumers' co-operative movement, were weak. In addition the power of government usually resided in the same minority as that which controlled the economy.

Since the 1930s there have been very marked changes with regard to state intervention, government policies, the greater influence of organized groups, social policy reforms, and the quickened pace of industrial expansion, and these have meant that structural change in the economy has acquired quite a different content from what it would otherwise have had. Structural change has become increasingly reconcilable with a rapid rise in the standard of living, the possibilities of choice, and security for the individual. Above all, it has made the distribution of the increase in welfare more equitable. While it is true that, on the average, the standard of living had previously risen in step with the growth of industry, and that rough estimates often speak of the tripling or quadrupling of the standard of living in Sweden between 1870 and 1940, a typical and rather dark feature was that the rise was so unevenly distributed. Those in employment benefited, though there were great inequalities between them as well, the healthy and the active gained, but not the sick, the elderly, or the unemployed. It was only with full employment and the welfare policy launched in the 1930s and extended in later years that a rise in the standard of living was brought about in which all could share, through more equitable distribution. The maintenance of full employment and new techniques have also been associated since 1945 with a more rapid expansion of industry. This combination, of industrial growth, a rapid rise in the standard of living, a continuance of a social welfare policy, and strong trade union organization among the large groups of wage earners, has made it possible to look forward and to plan for the future with great hopes.

CHAPTER II

THE NEED FOR CO-ORDINATION

Two characteristics distinguish the sweeping structural changes in the economy that have occurred both in Sweden and in most other industrial countries since the 1930s; first, the rapid growth of the public sector and, second, the integration in the private sector, both through the move to large-scale enterprise and the spread of a system of organized groups. The changes in structure have largely occurred without any planned co-ordination, but the Government has been forced, mainly for social policy reasons, to regulate structural changes at a number of points in order to reduce their effects on groups that are particularly exposed or occupy a strong political position. Government intervention has often assumed forms, such as import controls or export subsidies, which have had a distorting effect on competition both at home and in international trade, and they have not been evolved as part of a systematic economic policy. This has meant that in most cases the conditions simply do not exist for governing structural change in the economy automatically, through free competition between a large number of producers on the basis of prices set in world markets. Instead, change is affected by Government intervention and regulations, by organized groups in the economy, and by the large enterprises, all of which may have a wide variety of objectives in mind. In these conditions it is necessary to have a *programme* to provide a basis for policy interventions, so that our available resources can be utilized in the best way and wrong investment decisions and distortions of the economy can as far as possible be avoided.

There are in our view a number of factors which indicate that the transformation of the structure of the economy will be much more rapid and sweeping in the future than in the past. There is therefore a greater need now for a development plan based on a programme of action for economic policy. Much greater flexibility will be required if Sweden is to maintain her position as an economically well-developed country, and every prospect of making the economy more efficient must accordingly be exploited. This will be facilitated if a flexible, long-term plan exists to provide a basis for action and stimulate production, for it will reduce the risk of landing in situations in which short-term measures have to be improvised which tend to become permanent and in the long run can have a distorting and hampering effect on production. At the same time, a plan will improve the prospects of a more steady and harmonious development of Swedish society as a whole.

SOME IMPORTANT FACTORS AFFECTING STRUCTURE

The structure of the economy is influenced by a number of factors, some of which operate continuously and over a long period, while others are more specialized and short-term in character. Changes in international trade, direct controls introduced by the Government, by other agencies of society or by organizations in the economy, new inventions and technical discoveries, or changes in consumers' tastes and in demand, have a direct influence on the structure of the economy, and necessitate change. Other phenomena operate more indirectly, for example domestic and foreign political events, legislation or other action by the Government or by other social agencies, and changes in the size and composition of the population. Sometimes these factors reinforce one another and thus hasten movement in a particular direction. In other cases, again, they may work against one another, and make it difficult to discern long-term trends.

Political developments are particularly significant both for the intensity and direction of economic activity. Thus, in our view, the struggle for power between East and West is a fundamental explanatory factor underlying hothouse developments in technology, current international economic integration, and the newly-awakened interest in aid to the poor countries. This struggle is important too, as of course is that between other national group interests, for the level of employment and the rate of economic expansion. The tension between East and West appears likely to persist in the foreseeable future, and since this encourages great efforts by each side to force the pace of economic development, both for the purpose of showing the superiority of its particular system through expanding peaceful contributions at home and abroad and for strengthening the foundations of military preparedness, it seems likely that the world economy will continue to grow and that the prospects of maintaining full employment should therefore be bright.

Space does not permit a discussion of all the factors that can influence the structural development of the economy and ought therefore to be taken into account by economic policy, and we shall confine ourselves to drawing attention to some of the factors which we consider fundamental:

(a) developments in techniques (research and the application of its fruits), which will result, presumably at an accelerating rate, in new discoveries and inventions that transform the structure of the economy. By techniques is here meant technique in the widest sense, including organization;

(b) endeavours to liberalize international trade, which can be expected on the one hand to have short-term structural effects through drastic alterations in the economic conditions of different countries, but which on the other hand will probably necessitate structural adjustments in the long run because international political and other events can then work their way more rapidly through to domestic and export markets;

(c) the growing realization in the rich countries of the need to assist the poor countries in their efforts to develop. Aid must lead to an enormous increase in the exchange of goods with these countries and to adjustments in the structure of the economy;

(d) changes in demand and in buying habits as a result of the faster increase in productivity and in the standard of living, facilitated, for example, by changes in techniques.

DEVELOPMENTS IN TECHNIQUES

Nowadays research is increasingly conducted on a large scale, on the principle that a problem can be solved if only sufficient resources can be devoted to it. Here a small country such as Sweden, with limited resources for research and relatively small production units, faces awkward problems. Swedish enterprises are frequently too small to be able to afford an extensive research programme, and they are therefore largely thrown back upon trying to use the fruits of research in other countries and large firms, in so far as these are available. Even this necessitates considerable resources. In certain particularly vital sectors of the Swedish economy an independent research effort is, however, needed, and this has exercised pressure towards the formation of large enterprises or greater co-operation between different firms, and also between the Government and private industry. This affects the competitive position and behaviour patterns of business firms, and leads to successive changes in the structure of the economy. However, the results of more intensive research work are of even greater importance for the future structure of the economy and of society, for they relate to better methods and aids for production and distribution, or completely new goods and services, which exert their main influence on the structure of sectors and industries already in existence. In addition, however, new goods and services are for various reasons most often developed in the first instance by existing enterprises. It is reasonable to assume that this will continue, but at a faster pace. The more resources that are devoted to research, the more rapid and more fundamental are the results that emerge; and the higher the level of knowledge and the more general the technical awareness, the more extensive are the results which can be obtained.

INCREASED INTERNATIONAL INTEGRATION

The European trade groups

The growing requirements of large-scale production and specialization have meant that the importance of freer trade and greater division of labour, particularly between small and medium-sized countries, has become increasingly prominent in economic debate. The question itself is of course neither new nor particularly original; free trade is an old subject of controversy. What is new and original is instead that there has been some success in achieving concrete results—perhaps not least because of the pressure from the power bloc in the East—in the form of the European Economic Community (EEC, The Six) and the European Free Trade Association (EFTA, The Seven). The former (EEC) is a fairly tight organization—a Customs Union—between countries in close geographical proximity to one another and with traditional and lively economic links. Its aim is as much political as economic integration, even if the former has not yet found much concrete expression. It has a strong tie with the North Atlantic Treaty Organization (NATO); EFTA is a looser association, a free trade area with a membership that is geographically and economically rather widely dispersed. It was created primarily as a bargaining counter in relation to The Six and it does not aim at any political integration. Within The Six the tendencies to integration have proved very strong, with extensive rationalization and an increase in efficiency as a result. Developments and integration are taking place more rapidly in this market than within the EFTA area, and this is leading to a more rapid increase in production which is calculated to arouse some disquiet in EFTA quarters.

It is impossible to assess in detail the long-term effects on the Swedish economy of this international economic co-operation. In general terms, it seems probable that it will lead to more intensive competition. The effects ought further to be most evident for those branches which enjoy the greatest protection against imports to Sweden or which encounter the stoutest obstacles to imports in other participating countries. Since, apart from agricultural products, tariffs are as a rule low for raw materials, it is manufacturing industry which can in the first instance expect increased competition in domestic markets when customs duties are swept away. At the same time, however, industry will obtain the advantage of the other EFTA countries abandoning their customs and import controls. In

25

practice the existing disposition of markets is often of great importance: the more an industry is concentrating on export markets the more it is likely to benefit. Conditions do, however, vary from firm to firm. In many cases it may be possible to develop an export market which had previously not existed. But this must be based on the circumstances of the country and, in the case of Sweden, industrial activity ought primarily to be based on raw material resources such as timber and ore, on a high technical and cultural standard, or on a combination of these.

Within EFTA, in contrast to The Six, sectors of the economy other than industry are not as a rule directly affected by the agreements entered into so far. However, import firms ought to be favourably affected by the tendency to purchase more abroad, and shipping ought to benefit as well. Within EFTA it is also very unlikely that agriculture can be kept outside the free trade area in the long run. More intensive contacts of a different kind also follow in the wake of a growth in international trade: more business trips, increased tourist traffic and so on. This affects the service industries. The increasing efficiency of industrial production which follows from free trade means a more rapid rate of progress, which affects other sectors of the economy too. How rapidly this progress occurs will depend to a large extent on the economic policy that is likely to be followed. Structural transformation can be expected to be more rapid in future as a result of the increased trade liberalization, and this would be even more likely if the EEC and the EFTA groups were to combine. However, it is important not to exaggerate the rate of change and its scope. No economic revolution is likely as a result of more liberal trade within Western Europe, but the effect on economic growth will probably be favourable.

The consequences of liberalized world trade

Although economic integration in Western Europe will be of very great importance for the future of the Swedish economy, we consider this will be affected even more by developments outside the 'Western World'. The Soviet Union and other communist countries have shown they are quite capable of a significantly faster rate of economic growth than the EFTA countries and the USA. To be sure, it is still possible to use import controls to insulate domestic markets from the direct competition of government trading by the Eastern bloc; but it cannot be avoided in foreign markets, particularly in relation to the poor countries. The majority of these have now become conscious of their economic and social backwardness, their unexploited possibilities, and the discrimination against them by the rich countries, and they are making ever louder demands for justice in economic affairs and assistance in developing their national assets. The political tension in the world means we can assume that these demands will increasingly be satisfied and, as we shall develop in subsequent chapters, we consider this to be very desirable. Grants and credits by both power blocs will hasten the industrialization of these poor countries. It will not be as easy in future as it has been in the past to insulate ourselves from the under-developed countries and prevent the import of their cheap goods to the Swedish market. It appears probable that international economic co-operation will increasingly be directed towards the liberalization of trade with these countries as well. An important step in this direction has already been taken.

One important undertaking for the newly formed Organization for Economic Co-operation and Development (OECD), which consists of eighteen West European countries plus the United States and Canada, is to concern itself with the aid which the member countries give to the poor countries. The non-industrialized countries are already an important market for Swedish exports, and as they continue to industrialize they will steadily become more important as purchasers of capital goods. Thus Sweden cannot escape these trends.

If she liberalizes imports of goods from the poor countries it may mean that several sectors of Swedish industry will find it very difficult to survive competition. This applies not only to raw material producers or manufacturers of cheap mass-produced semi- and finished products such as textiles, which have traditionally been regarded as the main export articles of the poorer countries. If the pressure of population prevents wages and the standard of living in these countries from rising in step with the increase in productivity, they may at a later stage constitute a serious threat to quality production as well. This is already the case with Japanese exports.

CHANGED CONSUMPTION HABITS

The most important positive result of these factors that influence the structure of the economy would be a higher standard of living. But the rise in material standards, which expresses itself in people having more money to spend, or obtaining more for their money than they did previously, also affects the shape of the economy. Consumers' opportunities for satisfying their needs increase along with their incomes. Nor is it only traditional needs such as food, clothing and housing which can be better provided for than before; new needs develop as well, and people endeavour to satisfy these too. As incomes rise, a larger proportion of income tends to be spent on goods

27

which satisfy these needs, such as motor cars, television sets, domestic appliances, articles for leisure pursuits, or services such as travel, repairs, and eating in restaurants. Rising standards also make increasing demands on social services. Demands for education, for care of the sick, for housing and roads, for town planning, for leisure facilities and outdoor activities grow in step with, and partly as a result of, the attempts to satisfy the wants mentioned earlier. Shifts in consumption patterns affect the structure of society and of the economy, and these must be adjusted to provide the activity which matches the demands of the consumers.

THE NEED FOR A PROGRAMME FOR ECONOMIC POLICY

Political and economic events in the world happen swiftly, and the situation is in a constant state of flux. If we are to be in a position to preserve and improve the material standard we have achieved and to safeguard that personal security which people in general can now feel, thanks to full employment and the major social reforms, it is not enough simply to accept the fact that perpetual changes will necessitate structural adjustment. We must anticipate these problems and take steps to facilitate adjustments so that we can benefit by them and at the same time safeguard the interests of the persons affected by them as much as possible. Short-term economic policy, which is geared primarily to anti-cyclical devices, must therefore be supplemented by more long-term guiding lines for the development of the economy and of society, in brief by a programme for economic policy.

It has often been argued that the element of planning involved in such a programme could not be of any particular service, since the future cannot be foreseen with sufficient confidence. While admitting this difficulty, which resides in our ignorance of the future, we wish to stress that we are not seeking planning of a kind which presupposes that the future can be anticipated in detail. Our programme aims instead at drawing up certain broad lines of development within which the various units will operate.

CHAPTER III

VALUES AND GOALS

An economy and a society do not develop in accordance with any inviolable natural laws. On the contrary, they are the result of human action, and this is conditioned by the ambitions and value judgments of the individual. These in turn are moulded by social, economic and political influences in a complex process of interaction. In so far as the values are common to large groups of people, it is possible to co-ordinate their aspirations in the interests of efficiency, and change can then be influenced in a systematic manner. Our observation that the structure of the economy will undergo change in the future, as it has in the past, does not mean that we should simply have to accept change in a passive way and adjust to given circumstances. We can instead select the content which we wish these changes to have, and to a large extent we can determine their direction and outcome. But we must then be clear in our minds how and why we are choosing, in other words we must make our choice consciously and deliberately.

OUR VALUES

We begin from values which are generally accepted in the labour movement. These values require that a trade union programme for economic policy must aim at providing people with a richer and fuller life, with the right and resources for the individual to choose his training and his job according to his interests and his endowments, his consumption, and his 'way of life'. Within this broad framework seven 'partial values' can be said to be fundamental.

Freedom

We wish to live in a democratic society and under the rule of law. One of the basic principles of such a society is that the freedom of the individual ought to be left as inviolate as possible. Only if the individual citizen through his actions violates the rights of other persons or groups, or so harms himself that he can be considered to become a burden to society, ought intervention to take place. Another basic idea is that the rules, in the form of written or unwritten laws and customs, which form the framework for our actions shall apply equally to all, irrespective of occupation, income or

29

ancestry. In our view it seems obvious to transfer these values to the economic sphere as well. The following requirements then follow from these values. The content of the measures designed to promote structural change must not be such that strong centres of economic power develop in society, which can arbitrarily and selfishly 'steer' the direction of consumption, control the emergence of new enterprises and influence the determination of incomes and employment. An economy with a structure of this kind would in the long run constitute a threat to the democratic evolution of society.

It is of course true that complete freedom for everybody in all things can never be attained. The object should, however, be to increase the total 'sum of equality and liberty' in society. From this point of view limitations on the freedom of action of particular groups may also be desirable and necessary. If channelling demand in a particular direction were to contribute markedly to facilitating planning by enterprises, and make possible simplifications in both production and distribution, and this could benefit consumers in the form of lower prices, it could perhaps be tolerated. Such direction already occurs in practice, in the first instance by price fixing, but also through business advertising and other sales promotion measures, and through administrative decisions by Government and other authorities. In the same way, limitations on the freedom of action of producers can often help to increase efficiency. When Government has intervened here it is not the question of pure technical efficiency which has generally been uppermost, however, but rather the desire to protect various weak groups, i.e. the Government has been attempting to extend freedom in another sphere, such as that of consumers, or to favour certain groups of producers at the expense of other business interests.

Security

The need for security is the strongest impulse behind the development of the modern welfare society. It manifests itself on both the material and on the spiritual or psychic plane, in the need for security as a basis for physical existence as well as in the need for a secure anchorage in society and in relations with other people. Freedom has little meaning for those who do not possess security. Bourgeois, and in particular liberal, ideologies have often tried to see a conflict between security and freedom, and still more between security and efficiency. The utilitarian psychology of the eighteenth century, which provided the basis for this ideology, interprets human beings as fundamentally calculating and selfish; and on this view the only spurs to increased effort are intense competition, insecurity, and the prospect of material gain. This psychology is at the root of the doctrine of free competition and its superiority, and of the whole view of society on which modern capitalism has been founded.

However, the modern social sciences see in security a very important factor in the development both of the individual and of society. Human beings are regarded primarily as social creatures, whose complicated and often irrational character and behaviour develop through close interaction with their surroundings, and who have a great need of secure relations with this environment in order to live harmoniously. Security is also a prerequisite of liberty and efficiency.

Democracy

In our culture a democratic organization of society has a value of its own as well as being the basis of liberty, security and equality. It does seem, however, that a very real conflict can arise between the search for the preservation and extension of democracy and the need for efficiency. It arises in two ways. In the first place, an improvement in the organization of the economy, of administration and organizations, is often tantamount to a concentration and centralization of responsibility and power. The gulf between private individuals and the decision-making bodies widens accordingly, contact becomes more difficult, and people lose both the prospect of, and interest in, making their influence felt. In the second place, the very process of democratization itself, combined with an improvement in the functioning of the social mechanism, leads to some elimination of the causes of conflict in society and thus to a falling-off of interest in participating in the community in one form or another. This process is a vicious circle; the continuous process of social integration softens the clash of interests and thereby one of the strongest inducements to political and trade union work. This in turn reduces the possibilities of decentralized organization, and so on.

The democratic forms for distributing power and responsibility may be preserved, but the real content can be successively diluted if many private citizens no longer participate actively in, and feel responsible for, economic and political decisions. There is undoubtedly a conflict here, on the one hand between the rigid and strongly centralized administrative forms to which the satisfaction of a pure efficiency criterion increasingly leads as the economic, social and administrative problems become more complicated and, on the other hand, the democratic requirement of the influence and responsibility of the many. If democracy loses its real content the possibilities of freedom, security, and equality which it provides can be lost. Even if the leaders are not deliberately seeking dictatorial powers, the frequently irrational and incalculable actions of the citizens must,

31

when the democratic basis is lost, appear as an obstacle to effective planning and administration, which must be counteracted and in the last resort eliminated.

This is not to say that the conflict cannot be resolved. It is not possible in this context to analyse in detail the points at which a clash with the requirement of efficiency really cannot be avoided, and the modifications of this requirement which may then become necessary. In certain cases the problem can probably be resolved through developing new forms for collaboration and influence. In other cases greater efficiency could probably be achieved equally well by taking steps to arouse the active interests of those at the lower levels as through centralization. What we wish to stress is that in the process of increasing efficiency we must be unceasingly vigilant about these problems. The broad lines of development for social policy, the economy and the activities of the organizations must of course be drawn up by the small minority to whom this task has been delegated, but this must take place through a fruitful process of interaction with the opinions of the members and of society at large if these persons are not to run the risk of suddenly losing their democratic foothold. The very choice of these persons has of course always been an essential form for this inter-action; among the possible parties and candidates those are chosen who correspond best with the general wishes and values that are 'in the air'. But this requires that there really should be some fairly well-conceived wishes and values 'in the air'. For the other necessary aspects of this cross-fertilization too it is essential to have the individual members of society taking part in political and trade union activity, so that opinion can crystallize about the many fundamental questions that come within the scope of these broad programmes.

The technically efficient economic and administrative apparatus we are seeking must therefore build on the foundation of a living democracy which is supported by the will of the people, and not on a growing bureaucracy within Government administration, industry, and the organized groups. This means that in every particular case where some measure is being planned the possibility should be examined of leaving part of the direct right of decision to the member citizens. In practice, such deliberations can often lead to an alternative being selected which is not always the one that immediately appears to be the most efficient in the technical sense.

Greater equality

A further equalization of incomes between different groups in society and a more equitable distribution of property are in our opinion desirable. This is essential if the 'equality of liberty' for which we are striving is to become possible. Against the background of this value, the structure and functioning of the economy should be moulded in such a way as to ensure that equalization of this kind does occur. More precisely, it means that there should be a check on strong groups or enterprises that occupy such a 'strategic' position that they can obtain 'unfair' economic advantages in the form of monopoly profits and rewards for labour services which are not reasonable in relation to the difficulty of the task and its value. It is also desirable to avoid an economic structure through which property 'automatically' becomes concentrated in the hands of a few persons or groups, e.g. by surpluses being retained in 'old' firms or all investment in 'new enterprise' taking place through them.

The distribution of wealth does of course involve both a problem of justice and a problem of power. An attempt has been made to solve the problem of justice via tax legislation, but it has not been possible in this way to equalize the property gains which the process of economic expansion creates through the growth of, and the rise in the value of, productive assets. Power has also been contained through the extension of national economic and social policy, but it still remains a fundamental problem. When the right of ownership and the possibilities of an automatic concentration of capital are restricted through tax legislation, ways have been found in the private sector of separating ownership from economic power, so that the latter can be preserved even if the former is in part lost.

Free choice of consumption

Business firms and the activity they pursue ought to be for the benefit of the consumer, and not for that of the owners or others employed in production. This means that the manner in which the economy does or ought to function, and the most appropriate structure for it, must be judged primarily from the point of view of the consumer. The consumer's interest is a progressive feature of the economy. The efforts consumers make to satisfy their needs provide the impulse to change, whereas the interest of the producer is often the conservative one of preserving the *status quo*. It is, however, true that most people are not solely consumers, but are also active as producers in one form or another. Since the consumer's interest is diffused among the whole range of products, the interest of the producer can often manifest itself much more strongly. Thus it has sometimes been politically necessary to find a compromise between these opposing interests, or in other and fairly frequent cases—at any rate in the short run—to choose a solution which aims in the first instance at safeguarding the producers' interests.

C

33

In general, and on a long term view, however, it is the interest of the consumer that ought to be promoted. This does not only mean that consumers should obtain the goods and services produced in economic activity at as low prices as possible. Goods and services must also be produced in those quantities and qualities that the consumer demands, and they must be kept available for him at the time and the place that he wishes. If these problems of adjustment are to be solved, consumers must in some way be able to influence the actions of business firms, and business must adjust to these wishes. This means that the resources of production must in the first instance be devoted to the expanding sectors of the economy, by which we mean not only those sectors which are expanding in the technical sense, but those which, on a long-term view, have favourable prospects of selling their products at home and abroad.

Social balance

A large part of our needs cannot, however, be satisfied adequately through the direct choice we make as private consumers, but must instead be satisfied through social decisions and activities. This applies to the 'basic investment', public services and consumption for which the public sector is responsible, particularly with regard to education and research, social care and culture. These needs and their satisfaction occupy a very prominent place in our values, particularly because of the special connection which they often have with the security of the individual. At any particular time it may naturally prove very difficult to strike a balance between these needs and the more private wishes of the consumer. But, as a general rule, we would argue that greater significance ought to be attached to these 'public' needs, in other words that a larger share of the growing resources of production should be devoted to their satisfaction. This means that we endorse a continued rapid growth of the public sector in our economy.

This growth is all the more justified, since the needs which will be catered for in this way are many times more essential for society and the individual citizen than large areas of private consumption. Does any one really prefer a motor car to a good school education? In addition, these needs are often derived precisely from the expansion of the private consumption of goods and services which promote demand in the public sector, e.g. motor cars require roads, domestic appliances require electric power, and so on. It would be unfortunate in the extreme to create a lack of social balance through permitting free 'welfare consumption' to blossom, without at the same time also ensuring the rapid expansion of education, social care, culture, roads, and power stations.

34

International solidarity

A fundamental aspect of the values which underlie our view of distributive questions is that solidarity must be an international concept, and apply in particular to the poor countries. The extension of solidarity in this way does, however, pose very difficult problems, not least with regard to the structure of the domestic economy. Thus a rapid expansion of industry cannot be achieved in the underdeveloped countries if they do not have freer access for their raw materials and simple industrial products to the markets of the rich countries, in order to earn foreign exchange for the purchase of capital goods needed for their industrial expansion. At the same time they must be permitted to protect their own infant industries against the overwhelming competition of the more efficient industries of the rich countries. This raises structural problems for the economies of our own and other industrial countries on a scale which people have not so far been prepared to try to solve. In the countries of the Western world people are as a rule aware that very strong efforts are needed to solve the problems of the poor countries. It is not sufficient simply to organize free trade. But the most important of the measures which we consider necessary has not yet been taken, namely that a conscious endeavour should be made to adjust the structure of the economy to a larger volume of trade with the poor countries. This also will confront the Swedish economy with considerable problems of adjustment.

OUR GOALS

A rich and meaningful life, such as that we are seeking on the basis of the values we have discussed, cannot be created without an expanding material foundation. The first general goal must therefore be that in future economic policy is devoted still more to growth and increased productivity. This requirement, it is true, is not quite so urgent as it used to be in the most advanced industrial countries. Indeed, it may even be questioned whether, in the light of the production which has already been achieved in the highly industrialized countries, it really is necessary to continue to argue so strongly in favour of efficiency and the need for further rationalization. Is it not the case that, for the first time in human history, we can afford to attach less importance to efficiency and rapidly rising production? A viewpoint sometimes expressed in current discussion is that it is now time to 'take things a little easier'. It is argued that the tempo of work is very feverish and that the whole pace of life has increased, and this, so it is said, has harmful effects. Technocratic ideals of efficiency and old-fashioned views about the importance of 'the in-

35

crease in production' have, it is argued, come to dominate and direct our actions far too much. The time ought now to be ripe for devoting increasing attention to the private individual and his personal needs, environment, and problems.

Let us repeat that, from our starting point, the objective of economic activity must be to give individuals the resources which enable them to attain greater liberty and satisfaction in their lives. In our view this objective does not conflict with the requirement of efficiency. The casual connection between the demands of modern working life and the structure of contemporary society on the one hand, and the prevalence of particular physical and mental pathological pictures on the other, is much more complicated, and it also depends on other factors besides those allowed by the static and antiquated psychology which provides the source for these ideas. Mental insecurity in a dynamic society is probably more important than the pace of work as such for people who have grown up with the ideology and traditions of a more static order of society. The same is true of that insecurity which is a necessary result of the spread of the competitive ideology to various branches of social and cultural life. These difficulties can be expected to recede when group norms and behaviour patterns have had time to adjust to more flexible forms of society.

Moreover, there is no simple relationship between rationalization and high productivity on the one hand, and mental stress at work on the other. The latter depends largely on the technical nature of work processes. In the same way as the first steam-driven machinery two hundred years ago introduced the mechanization of simple physical tasks, today, with the first electronic brains, we stand on the threshold of mechanization of routine but often tiring mental work. At the same time, we take the view that a dynamic society as such may have some positive significance for human contentment. It can create interests, and give the individual scope for participating in society in a useful way and making a personal contribution to the life of the community. A dynamic society in which efficiency is increasing and the economy is growing can thus well be, and ought to be, associated with a concern for the human factors. This can be done by so directing the structural and cultural activities of the community that they create secure human relationships as well as material security. At the same time, automation should be used to avoid the excessive mental pressure of work, in the same way as mechanization has already succeeded in avoiding most of the excessive physical strain. In both instances a modern trade union movement has an important part to play.

Further, it is far from being the case that we require efficiency and technical advance solely for the purpose of creating a dynamic, contended society. If we include greater leisure in the concept of a richer life, this will put a greater burden on the productive capacity of the economy. The rise in demand resulting from shorter working hours must be met by a more rapid rate of substitution of machinery for human effort. This necessitates a rise in investment, and means a further increase in competition for the factors of production. In these circumstances our resources will soon become over-strained unless every possibility for increasing efficiency is explored.

In any case, what would be the result if we were satisfied with a considerably lower rate of economic growth, if we were to 'take it easier'? Even if for the moment we disregard the fact that, as we have discussed above, the psychological problems are not so simple in fact, the dependence of the Swedish economy on dynamic international developments means that a unilateral damping down of the rate of growth would have serious consequences. If we in Sweden were to decide to take it easier and not develop at the same rate as other countries we would obviously lag behind, relatively speaking. But that would not be the end of the matter. When Swedish goods and production methods became more and more old-fashioned compared with those of our foreign trading partners, they would naturally be unwilling to purchase our products in the same quantities as before. Thus we would find it more difficult to pay for the goods we wanted to import from them. We might in the end have to try to manufacture substitutes ourselves. Our production resources would then be used less effectively than before, since we would not have the same possibilities for producing these products as the countries from which we had previously imported them. In the long run the price of our quieter life would not simply be a relative decline, internationally speaking, but an absolute reduction in material standards.

In addition to all this, the international solidarity mentioned earlier provides a very strong reason for continuing our economic growth. We can no longer confine our horizon to Sweden and other economically well-developed countries. The need for a larger contribution to help the peoples of the under-developed countries raise their standards of living has become more and more inescapable as the result of recent developments in world politics. It is both a crying economic and political necessity and a moral obligation. Even if we did have complete freedom of choice, it would not be proper for us to 'be content with what we have' as long as a large proportion of the population of the world lives at or near starvation level. It would mean that we were not utilizing our resources to the full, and were restricting our opportunities for helping less fortunate people in other countries. In the light of the competition that prevails between different political systems, it is clear that an active and realistic contribution to the development of the poorer countries is a matter of life or death for the future of democracy.

Our values and general starting-point thus lead to the requirement of continued economic growth and increased productivity. This objective can be stated more precisely in the following four points:

First, full employment must be maintained. It is not only an economic but also a social necessity that no human being should be made superfluous. At the moment it may seem that a growing economy and full employment are inextricably inter-twined. But it is not necessary to look any further than the United States and its labour market to realize that the problem may perhaps not always be so simple. Economic policy must unceasingly be directed towards creating this union of growth with full employment.

Secondly, the character of production itself is of great importance. In view of the multitude of social and private controls over the price mechanism nowadays, the criterion of private business profitability alone can no longer be allowed to determine, if indeed it ever could, what is to be produced. The community must ensure that productive resources are devoted to sectors which it appears most desirable to promote on the basis of the ruling political and social values. It is particularly important to achieve a 'social balance' between the utilization of the resources of production by industry and by the Government. Nor can the allocation of investment within the private sector be left competely free. The authorities must assist in various ways, so that private investment harmonizes with the long-term assessments of what are likely to be the expanding sectors of the future.

Thirdly, in connection with the character of production, attention must also be paid to the distribution of the results flowing from the improved use of the means of production. Those who participate in the process of production must be guaranteed a reasonable reward in relation to their efforts, and those who cannot, for reasons of old age, illness, or similar circumstances, make any active contribution must obtain a reasonable share of the fruits of production. The process of economic and social equalization must continue. We consider that aid to the under-developed countries is a particular part of the problem of distribution. Social integration in Sweden has been carried comparatively far, but the feeling of solidarity has only become international in a very sporadic way. Now, however, we have reached the stage in world development where we can no longer avoid carrying through a process of integration on a world scale of the same sort as that which has been achieved in the past few centuries *within* the economically most-developed countries.

Fourthly, as has been argued earlier, the structure and apparatus of production must be adapted so that the social and industrial environment takes more account of psychological, social and other values. While these cannot be measured precisely in money terms, they are important for the security of the individual and his adjustment to his surroundings, and thus they can also promote productivity in the long run.

CONFLICT AND HARMONY AMONG GOALS

Certain of our objectives or some of our values may appear irreconcilable when a specific decision has to be taken. The more we try to attain one end with particular means, the further we are from achieving another objective. A conflict of goals or of values then exists. If, for example, rapid economic development necessitates extensive and costly research, this can lead to strong concentrations within the economy, since only large firms have the necessary resources, and only large enterprises 'controlling' a significant share of the market find it profitable and attractive to devote resources to such work. A move in this direction could mean a conflict with the desirability of a free choice of consumption, more equalization of wealth, and the democratic dispersion of power in society.

In such situations of conflict there must be compromises, though it is hardly possible to determine in a general way and in advance which objectives and values will be given priority. All the same, it is important not to exaggerate the importance of the possible clash in particular situations.

The various objectives which we have set out for our economic policy programme are not in fact independent of, or isolated from, one another. Indeed they merge in the long run in one particular value: a 'better' society. The amount of the increase in production and the rate of growth of the economy depend on the way in which resources are utilized and allocated among different tasks. In turn, the amount and the spread of incomes among different groups depend on the volume and direction of production. But the amount and distribution of incomes influence the character of production and the rate of expansion. Finally, all these factors are of decisive significance for the opportunities people have for satisfying their needs. This influences their adjustment to, and satisfaction in, society, which in turn affects production, and so on. Here we can speak of a high degree of harmony among our goals; the better we can attain one of our goals the easier it is to achieve the remainder.

In this connection, something ought to be said in conclusion about the choice of means. Sometimes the means become objectives or 'goals' in their own right. Thus people speak about a low rate of interest or progressive taxation as though they were not only or primarily means to achieve a particular distribution of income, but also ends that ought in all circumstances to be upheld. It is necessary to be on one's guard against the rigidities in economic policy which can readily follow from such an outlook. If, for example, means such as those mentioned obstruct important objectives, such as a more rapid rate of economic growth, and at the same time the change in the distribution of income could be achieved by completely different methods, we ought of course to choose freely in the light of all these possibilities. Means which in one period could be unsuitable, for example, indirect taxation, can in a new situation appear appropriate for achieving justice in taxation. Values and goals remain fixed over the long term. But in any particular situation it ought to be possible to re-assess the means or methods in the light of these goals and values.

CHAPTER IV

THE TASKS OF ECONOMIC POLICY

MORE ADAPTABLE FACTORS OF PRODUCTION

If we are to be able to ensure full employment and a continued rapid rise in standards, the Swedish economy must be in the van in exploiting new techniques applicable to methods, materials, and finished products. The structure of the economy will have to undergo incessant change. This will necessitate the correct timing of investment to transform and direct the old apparatus of production to new tasks or the utilizing of depreciation reserves or expanding resources for the purpose of developing a completely new apparatus of production. Adjustments will also be made necessary by the anticipated changes in technique and in international trade policy, which not only open up new vistas for our economy but will also make it more difficult, if not impossible, to continue certain branches of activity. Resources previously employed there must then be channelled into new fields of activity.

In these circumstances, the way to attain the objectives we have suggested for economic policy must essentially be to mark out definite guiding lines for the desired evolution; these can be based in part on the conditions and values discussed in Chapters II and III. The factors of production must then be made more adaptable if they are to be at all easily managed in accordance with these guiding lines. The problem is to reduce to a minimum the *sluggishness in adaptability* which is inherent in every economic system. The maintenance of full employment is of course an essential condition for achieving such flexible adjustments, since increased adaptability is meaningful only in full employment conditions.

THE MEANING OF ADAPTABILITY

By adaptability we mean the ability and willingness to accept change —*the readiness to adapt*. It is not necessary for a factor of production actually *to be moving* for it to be considered adaptable, but simply that it *can* adjust when the circumstances for its utilization change. Apart from this, the concept of adaptability can refer to several different things. It is most frequently discussed nowadays with reference to the labour market and labour market policy. People then think perhaps of a worker who for one reason or another has terminated or will terminate his employment with a firm and is seeking the same sort of job in some other firm in another place. This is the concept of *geographical* mobility.

We encounter the same type of mobility when a firm moves from one place to another, or opens a subsidiary in a new place. But it is also conceivable that the worker is unwilling to look for or cannot obtain the same type of job as he had previously, but is willing or compelled to try a completely new trade. Perhaps in that case he might not even have to leave his old firm, but simply obtain a new job within that firm. A firm can also 'change its job' and 'move between branches' through changing its products or taking up new products. This we term *'functional mobility'*.

Finally, the adaptability of the various factors of production may be largely a function of time. Here we can speak about a *technical and temporal aspect* of mobility. There is a tendency in modern industrial society to substitute machinery for human labour services. Capital costs, and fixed costs generally, are becoming more and more significant. But this also means that capital becomes more fixed; it takes longer to disentangle it and make alterations or modernize. In other words, the mobility of capital through time is reduced. At the same time, however, machinery and other real capital tend to be replaced more rapidly than before. The economic life of machinery and buildings has in many cases been reduced. For other factors of production besides capital time enters as a significant factor in the discussion of adaptability as well. Thus the increased knowledge required of most trades today means that training takes rather a long time. Training both facilitates and obstructs functional mobility; it facilitates it between closely related trades, but makes it more difficult between widely disparate trades. However, the period of training can be reduced through more rational methods of instruction and through an improvement in training facilities.

INERTIA AND OBSTACLES TO ADAPTABILITY

In a modern economy there are considerable obstacles to the free movement of the factors of production. In the case of capital the primary reason for this inertia is that we have created a production apparatus which is durable; in the case of labour, change involves uncertainty and insecurity. The apparatus of production is constructed for the purpose of being able to produce various kinds of goods and perform various types of service over a period of years. It takes times to alter this apparatus, and of course it is also costly.

Among employees there is often some antipathy towards and

opposition to any change in the existing state of affairs. We all have some established habits which we cannot give up without a particular effort. Our settled circle of acquaintances, accustomed milieu, and the element of uncertainty and insecurity associated with any change, are all factors that hamper adaptability. The same is true of business firms or, more correctly, of businessmen. It is easier to follow old, well-worn paths, to manufacture the same products year after year, to put money into one's 'own' familiar branch, to lend money to the old 'reliable' customers than to experiment with completely new products, or turn towards new branches, markets and customers.

When it feels threatened the 'old guard' tries to avoid the losses and insecurity of change and preserve its position by taking counter-measures to prevent the 'new guard' from making inroads. Steps can be taken to protect capital already invested and to preserve a particular level of profits, e.g. through agreements between various firms. Sometimes the existing firm or firms have sufficient resources to buy up or ruin possible competitors through a temporary, but ruinous, price war. In many cases the wage earners can also have an interest in acting in a restrictive way in order to prevent a threat to their position and avoid the need to adjust. Frequently neither of these groups is strong enough by itself to hamper new developments; but they may combine, e.g. to obtain an increase in customs duties or to protect their spheres of interest against strong and perhaps overwhelming foreign competition in other ways.

The lack of knowledge and insight into actual conditions which is always present in practice constitutes another inertia factor. A particular person may be quite willing to accept something new, but he is prevented from making an effective adjustment because his previous experience and his particular skills are no longer 'marketable', and through his having difficulty in meeting the new requirements, whether because of a lack of mental and physical preparation, inadequate funds or for some other reason. People seeking work who are ignorant of the situation on the labour market can remain unemployed in one area while there is a shortage of labour elsewhere. In the same way the allocation of their resources by business men is hampered by their imperfect knowledge of profits, trends in demand and in other market conditions, and by inadequate economic and technical knowledge.

The structure of the apparatus of production itself can also contribute to strengthening inertia in the economic system. In many industries specialization and mechanization have been carried so far that the firms—the buildings, machinery, and labour—are equipped and trained for one or a small number of tasks. This facilitates efficient mass production, but it hampers reorganization for other activities. If, further, the apparatus of production is not well integrated, but contains a number of bottle-necks, adaptability is made more difficult. Even if the labour force does exhibit sufficient readiness to adapt, whether through learning new skills or through changing the place of work, this is of little help if the corresponding capacity is not available in training institutions and in the production of houses. The same is true of business firms. We cannot, for example, obtain the location of industry which the community desires if it does not have the resources to provide the necessary services in those places where firms are expected to go. In addition, Government and other public regulations can often make adaptability more difficult and delay or distort a process of structural adjustment, because they have often been devised for quite a different purpose and have originated without a thought being given to their effect on the structure of the economy.

One additional result of the occurrence of these various elements of inertia is that the pricing system cannot function smoothly, but becomes rigid and sluggish. A rigid system of pricing is in itself an element of sluggishness. Thus significant shifts can take place in demand, supply, and cost conditions without these being reflected in prices and in this way affecting the scale and direction of production. Fortunately, inertia in the economy is not sufficiently strong to bring about complete stagnation. Human beings feel the need for variety, and curiosity and the desire for adventure favour novelty and inspire change. As a matter of fact change—the feeling of movement and progress—is an essential feature of our contentment in society. But, in our view, the obstacles to mobility are sufficiently strong to impose serious limitations on the development of our economic, social and cultural standards unless specific measures are taken against them.

The advantages of increased adaptability on the part of the factors of production must not, however, be exaggerated. Rapid adjustments can also give rise to serious social and economic problems—an increased shortage of labour, the closing down of business firms, and a loss of production. It is not always economically profitable to maintain a very high state of readiness to adapt. Far-reaching specialization and division of labour usually mean such large efficiency profits that it appears far too expensive to build up an apparatus of production which can very quickly be switched to new tasks. A rapid turnover of labour can also be disadvantageous, in view of the decline in production which occurs in changing jobs and during the process of adjustment to new tasks. In the capital market as well, switching to and fro as a result of shifts in the structure of the economy can give rise to financing difficulties and lead to wrong investment decisions. When firms build up a large capacity to adapt in the form of large liquid reserves, this is not only very costly, but it can, if it becomes general, bring about a cyclical instability in the whole economy. In other cases some stability and resistance to rapid change can be a social asset and be of fundamental importance for satisfying and protecting other values than the purely economic. Certain of the regulations which the authorities have introduced must be assessed from this point of view, and may then be defensible, even if they were to accentuate rigidities in the economic apparatus. Regard to physical and mental health and well-being, for example, must be given priority over more crude economic values, and make acceptable some limitations on the adaptability that would otherwise be possible.

INDUCEMENTS TO ADAPT

The general conclusion of our argument remains, however, that the ability and willingness of the factors of production to adapt must be increased. A desire to change does not, however, develop on its own; some inducement, a 'push', is necessary to bring it about.

In the case of business firms, the push expresses itself primarily through changes in demand, and firms can respond either through changing their prices or adjusting their volume of production, or both. The considerable rigidity in price-fixing that prevails means that it is nearly always production that is altered as a consequence of a change in demand. This rigidity springs primarily from the fact that production is increasingly dominated by branded goods, which makes it difficult to compare prices and gives the business man a certain monopoly position, but also from the difficulty of calculating the optimum price. In this way changes in demand are a more effective instrument for directing structural change, since their effect is not offset by price changes.

The autonomous changes in demand are, however, often overshadowed by the efforts which entrepreneurs make to use advertising to influence demand for their own advantage. Advertising can of course be of some value to the consumer as a source of information about the variety of goods available in the market. To some extent it may also be economically correct to adjust consumption to production, which is of course the object of advertising, instead of vice versa, and for the purpose of avoiding what the consumer regards as an unnecessarily large variety of models. In other cases it can, however, operate in the other direction, by making possible a large variety of brands and fashion-conscious shifts in demand.

Hitherto the possibility of making profit through competition as a result of changes in demand has been the main means used in our economic system both for adjusting to changed external and internal circumstances and as a general driving force in the economy. The chance of making such profits tempts business men to explore new avenues and methods, while at the same time the struggle between the different economic units threatens those who cannot adjust to the changes that have occurred.

In general, it can be said that the greater the inertia elements in the economy, the less will be the return on the various measures designed to stimulate adaptability, and the stronger must be the 'doze' both of reward and punishment in order to bring about a change on the scale desired, in the direction desired, and at an appropriate speed. In other words, the more sluggish enterprises are, the greater must the changes in demand be in order to bring about a change in production. The changes in demand will instead be expressed in queues or in price changes. The same applies to labour. The greater the resistance to geographical and occupational mobility the greater must the wage differentials or other benefits be in order to bring about the transfer of labour, and the larger is the deficit and the surplus of labour which arises in various sectors and areas in connection with the continuing process of structural transformation.

As integration within the economy proceeds through the trend towards large enterprises which dominate the market and through the formation of organizations in the economy, the prospect of profit comes to be a two-edged weapon. One can either 'take things easy' and exploit one's monopoly position or devote the increased resources which integration gives to further development, with the chance of further profit but perhaps also with greater risks. The temptation to follow the former line has always been put forward as the great threat of monopolistic and cartel tendencies to economic development. To a large extent it is also a real danger in those cases where cartels have been created precisely for the purpose of avoiding structural change, but it must not be exaggerated in those cases where a large share of the market goes to one firm as a result of an expansive and successful development policy. The continued divorce between management and ownership in large firms is leading more and more to management's ambitions to achieve and maintain modern and well-conducted enterprises weighing more heavily than the short-term profit interest of the owners. The absence of intensive competition need not therefore be so devastating for structural change, in view of the managerial traditions and the values associated with it which have come to be accepted in Sweden. Business men are motivated by many other factors besides the purely materialistic

46

forces embraced by the narrow psychology underlying the ideology of competition.

MEANS OF PROMOTING STRUCTURAL CHANGE

Structural change can be brought about through many different forms of stimuli or coercion; indeed, one of the most burning political issues is which of these are to be given priority in economic policy. The means can be divided into the following three groups, though they can in practice overlap to some extent: (1) measures designed to promote competition, (2) economic controls and planning, (3) the creation of centres of countervailing power. These are examined in turn.

(1) *The uses and limitations of competition*

Middle-class political parties often argue that the sole economic task of Government is to remove the obstacles to, and create favourable conditions for, free competition. If only this state of affairs could be brought about, the economy would automatically develop the maximum efficiency through the race between different business men, in which the least efficient would inexorably be forced to the wall. No one could then charge a higher price than the others, for in that case he would sell nothing; nor could anyone sell at a lower price without having discovered some better method of production than his competitors, for in that case he would not be able to cover his costs and would be ruined. But if he *were* to discover a better method of production, all the others would be forced to use it as well and to reduce the price by the same amount, if they wished to sell anything in the future.

However, this theory of perfect competition and its method of operation is based on assumptions which are far too unrealistic in most branches and sectors for it to constitute even a useful approximation to this state of affairs. The theory assumes, for example, that there are a large number of producers of every good, but in reality the trend is towards large-scale production and concentration in a small number of firms. Further, it assumes some degree of similarity between the goods of the competing enterprises, whereas in practice business men try to achieve the greatest dissimilarity, both real and artificial, in order to avoid competition. It also presumes widespread price and quality consciousness on the part of the consumer, whose controlling power forces business men to compete. Yet the enormous variety of goods and complicated problems of quality in modern times make it difficult for the consumer to make a sensible choice. In addition, selling and advertising methods try

47

everything to counteract the little price and quality consciousness that does exist. As a matter of fact, the theory also presupposes mobility on the part of the factors of production, and that detailed knowledge of market situations by every producer and consumer which the measures for promoting structural transformation must aim to create.

The unrealistic part of the competitive ideology is not the assertion that competition is an excellent mechanism for directing and distributing the forces of production, but the assertion that it could operate as an apparatus of control, always giving the best possible result from the point of view of the consumer, provided society remains neutral and avoids 'manipulating' the system. But the truth is quite different. If competition to promote efficiency is to develop a strong Government, able and willing to intervene in order to ensure competition, is needed. Even under such conditions, however, one cannot be certain of obtaining an economy which functions as flexibly and automatically as the theoretical model of perfect competition. As has been shown above, the practical requirements for this are also lacking; nor would it be desirable in every respect to go as far. We can, however, try to promote appropriate and working competitive conditions for our practical needs in sectors suited to it. Competition of this kind can be brought about if the Government accepts it as one of the main aspects of its economic policy and systematically adopts measures for the purpose of making it work.

This does not mean that every type of competition is to be patronized. Competition, frequently intensive, is often found, even in a modern economy. It can occur on many planes, express itself in many different ways, and use many different means. But not all these forms of competition increase productivity or benefit the consumer in any way. Government policy must therefore be directed towards a special defence of those methods of competition which lead to savings in costs, reductions in prices, and in general to more efficient production and distribution, and to ensuring that the fruits of this competition really do benefit the consumer.

The main trouble with current competition is not that it is lacking, but that it takes place essentially through measures which raise costs, such as advertising campaigns and changes in models, while price reductions occur only infrequently. Attempts are made at the periphery to lure customers from other producers, but competition which might damage a vital nerve is avoided. It also appears probable that, in the absence of counter-measures, the effectiveness of competition as a factor helping to rationalize the structure of the economy would be further diminished in the future.

During the postwar period, with its relatively short and mild recessions and high average level of employment—a situation which we have assumed it will be possible to maintain in the foreseeable future—business firms have been able to build up large financial reserves. This makes it possible for them to 'last the pace' of competition longer than would otherwise be the case; this may have a good side to it, namely that structural changes need not be quite so drastic as they sometimes were in the inter-war years. But at the same time it means that old and outdated forms of enterprise and methods can survive longer. Moreover, business firms are more willing to hang on longer, because the share of fixed costs is growing and variable costs are becoming a correspondingly less important part of total costs. The present structure of the economy, where a small number of large firms usually dominate most branches, often makes it possible for these to prevent the emergence of competition from 'outside upstarts'. Technical developments will presumably accentuate the advantages of large-scale production further—particularly from the research and marketing point of view—and make it more difficult for new competitors or 'outside' goods to enter the market.

The decisive weakness of competition as a means of promoting structural change is, however, that economic policy can certainly remove obstacles to effective competition, but it can never force a business man to compete against his will. No entrepreneur competes for the fun of it, and business men have long since realized that it is only the consumer who benefits from their mutual competition, while they themselves only reap the losses and the insecurity. The strong emphasis on security in modern society makes it natural for business men to wish to defend theirs as well. It would be unreasonable to require that they alone should sacrifice their security in order to promote the smooth functioning of the economy. It is easy to understand why they may wish to follow the example of workers, farmers, and many other groups, and establish a secure position for themselves through solidarity and co-operation. Economic organizations of all kinds have in fact been formed during the postwar period, and their influence on prices and other aspects of competition is often of considerable importance.

This is not to say, however, that competition has to all intents and purposes been eliminated nowadays as a means of promoting change and efficiency in the economy. There are three areas in particular in which competition is still maintained on a scale large enough for it to be fundamentally important for structural change.

First, and most important, a large part of Swedish production is continually exposed to competition from imported goods, or is forced to compete with the exports of other countries. Secondly,

D

there is persistent competition from firms not governed by the private profit motive, particularly co-operative enterprises. Thirdly, important competitive impulses are continually arising from new firms and forms of production whose products are so superior to those of the old that those launching them consider that they have a good chance of capturing part of the market.

In all probability foreign competition as an inducement to structural rationalization will continue to increase in importance as the movement towards more liberal international trade continues and as Western European integration is accomplished. Its limitation lies in the fact that large parts of the economy must, for purely practical reasons, remain outside its influence. This applies in particular to the greater part of the building and construction industry and distribution. The activity of the Consumer Co-operative Movement is the most important factor in the competition between groups that typifies wholesale and retail distribution in particular. However, the movement's policy of expansion has largely depended on its ability to finance new investment itself, since a movement of this kind must preserve its independence of any outside financial institution. This has to some extent weakened the price competition it has been able to exercise, and in addition it operates outside the foodstuffs sector on a comparatively small scale. Rapid advances in technique have made new goods and new forms of production and distribution more common since the war than before, and in many cases foreign competition has also been an important impulse. But new ideas have usually come from existing enterprises, for the costs of research and development have generally been far too great for new firms, with little or no depreciation facilities, to be able to carry them. But this also means that the old enterprises can mould pricing policy in such a way as to retard structural change and avoid the need to incur losses on their investment in older products and forms of production.

In many ways competition would be an excellent means of increasing efficiency and promoting structural change in the economy. It avoids a mass of administrative trouble and social controls over the economy in a myriad of detail. Perhaps the greatest advantage of competition is that, more so than planned measures, it is regarded as an impersonal force, and the criticisms of those adversely affected by its results cannot be directed against any particular person or institution. Criticism of planned measures, on the other hand, can always find a target in those who undertook them, and thus it can much more readily be given a political bias. But the great weakness of competition is that it is difficult to create it. Despite these advantages, therefore, it is not possible to rely solely on competition for bringing about structural change. Very extensive use must also be made of other possibilities in order to increase efficiency. In addition, the lack of planning in a really competitive economy gives rise to much duplication of effort and waste of the community's resources.

(2) *Economic controls and planning*

Our strong scepticism regarding the possibilities of bringing about effective competition on a sufficiently large scale for it to be able to direct the process of structural change on its own does not imply that we consider we can shut our eyes to the great difficulties which confront the practical application of a more deliberately planned economic system. Even with improved methods of calculation and forecasting the risks of making wrong assessments, even if they are in total less than would be the case under free competition, are nevertheless considerable. Moreover, wrong judgments discredit the system immensely, while under competition they are considered to be a natural and useful consequence of the system and are accounted for by the 'free play of market forces'. In addition, it is possible that a planned economy may work against its own objectives, through the emergence of an element hostile to change in the form of a large, bureaucratic and conservative apparatus of controls.

If the fundamental objective set for economic activity is that the needs and wishes of the consumers have to be satisfied in the cheapest and best way, it is not sufficient simply to solve the technical problems of production and distribution. Planning must, in addition to this, and perhaps predominantly, consist of extensive market research and forecasting activity in order to ascertain how these needs and wishes can be expected to develop. It is only human if the planners react against incalculable shifts in consumers' demand and search for ways of facilitating their own work, chiefly through endeavouring to influence the direction of consumption so that it follows the plans, instead of adjusting the plans to the direction of consumption. This is particularly understandable since, as we have shown earlier, rational arguments can be put forward for *particular* adjustments of consumption to the conditions of production. In other words, the aim becomes the same as that which underlies modern advertising, but in a strongly centralized system the planners may have far greater resources of power at their disposal for this purpose. Under such conditions there is a risk that the direction of consumption will be steered far too much in accordance with the wishes of the 'planners'.

The strongest argument against an extensively planned economy is perhaps that it is far too sensitive to political pressures, and can therefore readily come to work counter to its objectives and in cer-

51

tain cases retard appropriate structural changes. To a very large extent this depends on the fact that it is burdened with great expectations concerning its efficiency.

The great and growing importance of the public sector means that administrative decisions have already become very widely used, along with other forms of impulse, for promoting structural changes. But economic controls are of great importance outside the public sector as well. If we want the economy to develop along somewhat different lines from those that would result if it were completely uncontrolled and dominated by advertising and profit, this can be achieved by regulating and co-ordinating the major lines of advance at the centre, while leaving the price mechanism and competition to take care of the details. Central control over the major features within the economy—what we call a co-ordinated economy—would therefore lead more quickly and more completely to the goals which we have set up. In addition, rapid progress in the techniques of communication has now made it possible to direct increasingly large and complex organizations from the centre.

(3) *Centres of countervailing power*

A third group of means for steering the structural development of the economy is the creation of centres of countervailing power. Here control is achieved either by the very existence of these centres or, most often, as a result of bargaining and agreements between power groupings in the market. Often there is a natural tendency for one party in the market to combine for the purpose of balancing a power on the other side. For example, employers also organize after the workers have formed a strong trade union movement. In other cases, however, the community must help to create, or itself act as, the countervailing power. The main difference between governing economic advance through countervailing power and controlling it by competition is that the power groups exist on *both* sides of the market, whereas competing enterprises operate on the same side. The centres of countervailing power are therefore less likely than business enterprises to discover a mutual interest in collaborating at the expense of a third party.

The labour market is the sector in which agreements based on countervailing power have the longest history, but in Sweden agricultural prices as well have long been regulated in a similar way. In the housing sector, the tenant and the property-owning associations form the centres of power facing each other, and in the field of credit policy the Government, through the Riksbank and the Swedish Credit Bank, has tried to establish some countervailing power against the interests of the private credit institutions. In this area the

National Pension Funds will come to have a dominating influence as centres of countervailing power.

The advantage of agreements over regulations is that the parties accept a responsibility for both internal and external developments which can never be imposed upon them through legislation and decrees. Further, agreements can be better adjusted in detail to suit existing conditions, while regulations, which must be armed with some sort of legal consequences, in many cases have to be made so general in character that they are either ineffective or leave considerable scope for administrative decision. The results which can be achieved through agreement are of course naturally limited to matters on which the parties consider they have an interest in agreeing. It is hardly possible to say anything in general terms about the way in which the creation of countervailing power does in itself affect the adaptability of the economy. This depends on the nature of, and the attitudes within, the organized groups, which generally provide the environment in which power and countervailing power emerge. They may frequently be dominated by protectionist tendencies, but they can also be influenced in such a way that they become instruments of structural change.

EVERY MEANS MUST BE MOBILIZED

Competition, controls, and countervailing power exist side by side in modern society, and we need to use them all to impart a stimulus and compulsion to structural change in the economy. In an economy of our type it is not possible to bring competition into being on a large enough scale for it to be able to govern the economy alone. Business men have long since seen through competition, and cannot be forced into more competition than they are willing to accept. Likewise, the public sector has grown so much in scope that an increasingly large part of production is thereby removed from the market economy. In this sector some form of planning is therefore inevitable in any case. Finally, centres of countervailing power exist as one of the facts of life in modern society, and as such they have their value. The object must therefore be to support competition by removing obstacles to the competition that arises naturally, more central control and planning and, above all, more conscious and systematic measures by the Government and, finally, greater scope and support to countervailing power and to experiments with new forms of bargaining policies.

The changes at which we are aiming relate both to the theoretical background and in particular the overall picture of the economy, and the co-ordination, planning and practical tools of economic policy that affect structural change. In this connection some revaluation on the theoretical plane is of some significance. In the past social controls have developed sporadically as the need arose, without any particular fundamental theoretical speculation about whether they fitted into the economic system. The march of events has not been matched by systematic theory, which has meant that popular discussion often deals with outworn and unrealistic concepts. This in turn gives a wrong notion of the real political differences of view that exist.

Thus we need a realistic theory if we are to have a correct understanding of developments. It is necessary as a foundation for planned action in the future. In an economy which is taken to be a 'free economy' without close controls on the part of the organs of society, it is easy to get into a situation where exaggerated importance is attached to the production of sundry individually identifiable consumer goods and services supplied by 'free private enterprise'. Competition between these business firms is carried on nowadays primarily through advertising and changes in models. Intensive advertising campaigns are used to convince the consumer that it is necessary for him to have the latest model of car, to use a particular detergent because it lathers so well or because it does not lather at all. At the same time as a surplus of various goods and brands for satisfying particular consumer needs arises, insufficient capacity exists in other, no less important, sectors, which are not suited to private enterprise and sale but where collective efforts are required. Education, legal assistance, care of the sick, urban planning, and housing are obvious examples. One of the important tasks of a more intensive and more efficient planning and control over the development of the structure of the economy must be to ensure that the needs which must be satisfied through social action are not neglected. In other words, we must ensure that an appropriate division exists between private and public activity, that what we have called a *social balance* prevails.

PART II

THE POLICY FRAMEWORK

CHAPTER V

THE BASIS OF A CO-ORDINATED ECONOMY

It is now generally agreed that short-run anti-cyclical policy should rely primarily on general weapons, supplemented by selective measures, to steer the economy by controlling the level of total demand. Fiscal and monetary policy in combination are then regarded as the main instruments of policy. Since there is always the likelihood that the economy will not behave uniformly in every sector, however, but that there will be excess demand in some sectors and deficient demand in others, this policy must be supported by a selective labour market policy which promotes adaptability.

This approach is also applicable in very large measure to structural policy. The same elements of inertia in the system which make it necessary to supplement general stabilization policy with selective measures also constitute a serious threat to our efforts to attain the long -term economic objectives which we have set up. The primary task of economic policy is then to ensure that our resources are allocated to the sectors with the best development prospects. This necessitates greater adaptability on the part of the factors of production.

The analogy between anti-cyclical and structural policy is by no means complete, however. Both the general and selective weapons of cyclical policy are by nature 'active', in the sense that they are intended to influence the economy in a certain direction, to have a damping effect in time of boom and an expansionary effect in time of recession. The idea is to use short-term measures to counter fairly rapid swings in economic activity, so that a certain degree of equilibrium is maintained in the economy. In our view long-term economic policy, on the other hand, ought not to be active in the same sense. Its most fundamental task is to remove the obstacles to, and promote and induce, the continuous adjustment of the economy to new circumstances. Thus our assumption is that a process of evolution which is as far as possible free—free not simply from detailed Government controls but free also of the sluggishness inherent in the system—is favourable to the forces of expansion and leads to the best economic results. The measures we recommend below do not aim in the first instance at pushing the economy in a particular direction mapped out in advance. That would be unreasonable, not least in the light of Sweden's great dependence on world markets and the rapid shifts which can occur as a result. What they aim to do is to strengthen the forces of expansion and remove the obstacles that stand in their way. This may, at a very cursory glance, appear to be a liberal view of the economy. But it differs in one fundamental respect from that form of liberalism which argues that the free forces function so well that no social intervention is necessary at all. We consider that this attitude is unrealistic, and we seek instead to create the environment for an efficient economy through constant new interventions.

To use the analogy from anti-cyclical policy, structural policies can be divided into general and selective measures. The establishment of a freer *credit market*, with a consequent increase in the mobility of capital, is a general measure. The selective element lies in the retention of priorities in granting credit for particular purposes, something which we think it will be difficult to avoid entirely in the foreseeable future. The reasons for this policy are both social and economic. The exceptional position with regard to the production of housing is by no means irrelevant to structural policy.

Tax policy ought in our view to operate in a general way. We propose that the subsidy elements in our existing system of company taxation should be eliminated. There should be no question of any selectivity, e.g. in the form of tax priorities for firms in particular branches or located in particular areas. *Foreign trade* policy, on the other hand, is one sector in which there are at present strong elements of selectivity. Certain products are given protection against imports, often for the most diffuse, random, irrelevant, and sometimes untenable reasons. In keeping with our sympathetic attitude to free trade, we recommend the successive removal of the remaining import controls, not simply in relation to the countries of the Free Trade Area but also to the world outside. In principle, selectivity has no place in international trade policy.

Finally, among the economic policy measures which are general in their effects, we shall consider *protection against monopolistic tendencies*. Legislation to promote competition must provide guarantees that the economy abides by certain rules of the game, and that the machinery does not cease to function as a result of monopolistic or other phenomena which restrict competition. However, anti-monopoly policy is not free from selective features either. Restrictions on competition are not considered harmful as such; the decision rests with the Freedom of Commerce Board, and since judgment involves selection this is significant from a structural point of view.

From what has been said it can be seen that structural policy measures are certainly both general and selective in character, but that the selective elements are of secondary importance. In certain respects we are anxious to see the selectivity in these measures further reduced. The more emphasis that is placed on the general effects of measures, however, the greater is the burden placed on labour market and location policies, and these by their very nature operate with selective methods.

The task of *labour market policy* in the context of structural change is to co-operate in bringing about the structural changes which a more liberal capital market, an expansionist tax policy, a systematic free trade policy, and an active anti-monopoly policy are intended to promote, and in addition to resolve those difficulties of adjustment which can be expected to arise if such a structural policy is to be realized. In this connection, *location policy* cannot be separated from labour market policy, since its task also is to give selective support to expansion. This is the same as saying that we do not approve of a location policy which aims at artificially spreading a differentiated economic structure, which works against the natural movement of labour away from sectors with no development prospects, and which arbitrarily erects obstacles to the influx of labour to the large urban areas. In this Part we shall discuss the constituents of the structural policy sketched here, beginning with the measures that are essentially general in their operation and then indicating the selective measures needed to supplement them.

CHAPTER VI

THE SUPPLY OF CAPITAL, CREDIT POLICY, AND STRUCTURAL DEVELOPMENT

The starting-point for the discussion in this chapter of the contribution which credit policy can make to stimulating structural change and progress is that, at least on certain assumptions, an increasing supply of capital improves the prospect of a more rapid rise in production and of a more efficient economic structure as well. The best use of the existing supply of capital is of course also an important question: the more capital is concentrated in expanding sectors, the more rapid is the rate of growth likely to be. In the light of the trends discussed in Chapter II, this latter problem must in our view be given greater attention in future. Even if a policy were to be pursued which led to the greatest possible efficiency under the existing credit market arrangements, these trends nevertheless pose an additional question. May it not happen that financing problems arise which it proves difficult to solve through the existing institutional arrangements, and which necessitate Government collaboration on a far larger scale than before? This particular point will be taken up at the end of the chapter.

CAN THE SHORTAGE OF CAPITAL BE OVERCOME?

The credit market has, in varying degree, been short of funds ever since the end of the Second World War, and the cheap money policy pursued until about 1955 probably accentuated the shortage. The typical state of the capital market thereafter can be described in the following way. Government borrowing showed a marked upward trend, as did finance for house building. A large proportion of Government borrowing could not be covered by the capital market, but took place through the Riksbank and the commercial banks. This led to a continuous increase in the supply of money held by the banks and the public, which made it easier for the banks to expand their lending for other purposes. At the same time the bond market was closed to purely industrial loans, largely in connection with the requirements of finance for housing. Despite this, it was sometimes not possible to remove building credits within the normal period, because final long-term loans could not be accommodated on the capital market and delays had developed in the disbursement of Government housing loans. In this situation the commercial banks considered they could not continue to grant new building credits on the same scale as before, and difficulties thus developed in the housing programme. Credit restrictions could, it is true, be applied to other sectors of the economy, but these of course need capital urgently as well.

As the Institute of Economic Research has pointed out in several of its reports, this shortage of capital cannot be ascribed to a declining propensity to save, but must instead be considered to relate to the very high propensity to invest. In this respect, the post-war years provide a graphic contrast to the 1930s, when there was a very good supply of credit in relation to investment demands, and a falling rate of interest. By contrast, as has already been indicated, all the important sectors of our economy have had large and growing investment requirements since the end of the Second World War, and in recent years investment plans in industry have been further increased through the liberalization of trade in Europe.

The Government has tried to solve the dilemma of the shortage of capital in the following three main ways:

(1) by stimulating personal savings—increasing the supply of capital through voluntary restraints on the increase in consumption;

(2) by a tighter fiscal policy—increasing the supply of capital through taxation, primarily of consumption;

(3) through credit restrictions—rationing the short supply and thereby reducing the demands satisfied in relation to the total loans wanted.

The policy has not been explicitly selective, in the sense of attempting to channel the flow of credit to private industry in the direction that might have been preferable in the light of the new market situation. But attempts to operate selectively have been all the more evident when Government borrowing had to be facilitated.

STIMULATING PERSONAL SAVINGS

Few, if any, measures since the war seem to have enjoyed such popularity in the general economic policy debate as attempts to increase the supply of capital and solve long-term economic problems through stimulating personal savings. The amount of personal savings is determined by a number of factors, and if measures to stimulate it are to be effective the stimulus must be such a powerful one that it may readily appear inappropriate on other grounds, for example distributive reasons. In so far as measures to stimulate savings do have any worthwhile total effect on the economy in the long run, this probably involves not so much a permanent increase in personal savings, and thus a better supply of capital, as a reduction in the demand for capital. The increased volume of savings means a restriction on the increase in consumption, and thence less private investment than would otherwise have taken place.

Measures to promote savings do not satisfy the requirement of providing scope for increasing exports and more investment through *temporary* increases in savings and reductions in consumption. If they could, it would be a fundamental long-term gain. But the likely long-term implications of savings reforms would instead be that any attempt to postpone or prevent price rises when exports increased or demand rose for other reasons would result in a fall in the level of demand, activity, and employment. This would conflict with our policy objective of full employment. If, on the other hand, the lower level of employment resulting from the decline in consumption that followed strong measures to stimulate savings was unacceptable, demand in the public sector or foreign demand could be expanded in order to stimulate total demand.[1] This would restore demand to its previous level, and the economy would return to its initial position, apart from some reduction in private consumption.

If measures to stimulate savings are thus likely to have the effect of restricting investment, other measures are available which operate more directly and can be more readily controlled, for example tax measures, or less protection to production which is in a weak competitive position. It is quite another question, of course, that some forms of savings may need some stimulus which would also affect the direction of the flow of capital and investment activity; but this point can be dealt with more appropriately in a discussion of the most efficient use of the available capital.

A MORE ACTIVE FISCAL POLICY TO INCREASE CAPITAL

We attach great importance to the close relationship between credit and fiscal policy. An active credit policy must be an essential supplement to other policy measures. Fiscal policy must contribute in the first instance to bringing about equilibrium in the economy, thus restricting the demand for capital and reducing the problems of priorities. A minimum requirement here is that Government income proper, in addition to the traditional depreciation payments by

---

[1] In this context we would like also to point out that a restrictive domestic economic policy which leads to an increase in foreign demand is intended to attract foreign exchange from other countries. We are unwilling to recommend such a policy, nor is it possible in the long run. Foreign exchange problems must be resolved through international co-operation.

agencies and funds, should not only cover expenditure on the current budget but part of the expenditure of the capital budget as well. When the overall economic position necessitates it, the Government's loan requirements must be reduced further until the total budget is balanced, or even over-balanced. Only in these circumstances can the problems which credit policy has to resolve be reduced to reasonable proportions. It also follows from this that a credit policy which is satisfactory from the point of view of productivity can only be carried out in conjunction with a more active fiscal policy.

We are, however, conscious of the political difficulties here. Behind the broad agreement in principle about the need for a 'strong' fiscal policy there is considerable disagreement about the ways of achieving it, whether through a real increase in Government income or through restrictions on expenditure. Our own view of this matter is evident from what has been said in Chapters II and III. It is also necessary to bear in mind that the strengthening of the budgetary position since 1960 has largely been connected with increases in incomes, partly inflationary in character, which have had a strong impact on the income side of the Government budget via the progressiveness of the income tax system. One additional sign that the stronger balance of the budget is partly inflationary is that the shortage of credit still persists to some extent. The reduction in Government borrowing has certainly given the private sector in general greater scope on the capital market, and it has been possible for the first time for many years to allow pure industrial loans to come forward on the bond market. On the other hand, the mortgage institutions have not been able to carry on their bond borrowing on a large enough scale, which has led to greater difficulties in converting building credits into long-term loans. This may possibly benefit 'the private sector' of the economy, and industry in particular, in the short term, but it is very doubtful whether it is also beneficial in the long run.

However, these difficulties confronting an active fiscal policy which is designed to facilitate a rational credit policy serve simply to emphasize once again how necessary it is. The National Pension Funds and suggested branch funds[1] are also important factors working in the same direction and helping to attain a higher investment ratio. We should be clear in our minds, all the same, that the existence of the Pension Funds may conceivably operate to make savings by the community through the budget appear less necessary than would otherwise be the case.

---

[1] These various funds are discussed in Chapter XIII.

CREDIT RESTRICTIONS TO RESTRAIN THE DEMAND FOR CAPITAL

From what has been said above it is clear that, so far at least, we have not succeeded in eliminating the shortage of capital, either through a voluntary increase in household savings or through a more active fiscal policy. In all probability we must expect the problem to persist. On this point our view differs from that expressed by the committee of enquiry into the credit market, which allowed itself to state its belief that the capital shortage would subside within a few years and the credit market would return to 'normal'.[1] In fact, a shortage of capital is probably an inevitable concomitant of full employment, though it may of course vary in intensity. It is important to ensure that the scarce supply of capital is used in the most efficient way in order to avoid the more negative effects in a full employment situation. All this implies that credit restrictions will continue to appear as one policy alternative.

The available capital has been rationed, partly through the Riksbank in the case of bonds, and in part by the private credit institutions themselves through 'voluntary' agreements arrived at with the Riksbank, under the shadow of legislation to regulate interest rates which has never been required. What effect has all this had on productivity? This question touches the problem of the most efficient utilization of the available capital from the point of view of productivity.

THE EFFICIENT USE OF AVAILABLE CAPITAL

(1) *Productive firms—expanding firms*

Competition for the available credit must be very great in a full employment society in which the resources of production are severely strained, and credit rationing is therefore likely to preserve the existing structure of the economy to a greater extent than would otherwise be the case. The shortage of capital does not simply stem from the inadequacy of total savings in relation to investment requirements, but also from the institutional confinement of capital to existing firms and branches of the economy. Thus the shortage would probably be less pronounced if a larger part of the capital flow could be directed to the most productive enterprises in each branch. Our thesis is that a more flexible policy with regard to interest rates, which could nevertheless be kept at a modest level, provided a more active fiscal policy were being pursued, would not conserve the structure of

[1] S.O.U. 1960: 16, Banklikviditet och kreditprioritering (Bank Liquidity and Credit Priorities).

the economy in the same way, but would open the credit market to those firms that can pay the prevailing price for credit. As a general rule these are the most progressive firms, best fitted for expansion. Interest rate and credit policy ought therefore to aim at making the capital market more flexible.

The next question is whether the most 'productive' firms (in the usual sense) ought really to be favoured as regards investment. It is sometimes argued that, on the contrary, investment in stagnating branches with a relatively low turnover per employee, or in low profit and low wage branches, would give a greater return than investment in branches of the opposite type. We consider that significant productivity gains could very probably be made simply through increasing investment in stagnating branches; this is easy to understand, not least because of the previous neglect of investment in them. But this is to look at the question more from a theoretical and technical aspect. The decisive points seem to be capacity and the outlook for demand. There is no denying that excess capacity often exists in stagnating branches, and that the prospects of eliminating it appear very remote. Nor could a large increase in investment designed to rationalize their structure avoid giving rise to additional capacity. The essential requirement in this context must surely be that the output made possible by new investment really can be sold. Without passing judgment on any particular case, we therefore consider that, as a general rule, it is probably wise to invest in rapidly expanding branches.

(2) *Credit institutions and the expanding firms*

Before endeavouring to judge whether the credit policy pursued in Sweden has helped the expansionary parts of the economy to grow, and thereby raise national productivity, it may be convenient to examine the normal pattern followed in granting credit. The overriding consideration as far as the institutions of the credit market are concerned is the security that a borrower can provide for a new loan, whereas the price, rate of interest, commission, etc., can be regarded more as given. The freedom of action of any one institution is much more limited, both as a result of Government controls and of agreements between the institutions themselves.

Events within the firms or sectors concerned may of course mean that risks occur in relation to the security offered, but the institutions can make no more reliable and realistic appaisals of the future prospects of different branches of the economy than anyone else. From this point of view, their concern should be to try to adjust their lending rapidly in the light of new trends in the economy. They naturally do attempt this, but there are nevertheless many sluggish

E

elements at work here of a personal or institutional kind. One basic characteristic seems to be that, when the institutions have once granted credits and thus acquired a stake in a branch to safeguard, and the branch subsequently stagnates, the usual investment problem arises. Should they make new credits available in the hope of salvaging earlier loans, or should these be deliberately sacrificed so that more money can be put into new and expanding branches instead? Here it seems that the natural fondness for accepted ways of thinking can readily be given too much scope. The point is illustrated by a recent study of the clothing industry, which makes it very difficult to understand how the commercial banks could support extremely weak firms by granting them almost unlimited credit facilities.[1]

In sum, there is often a lack of flexibility about the normal processes of lending, and this needs to be remedied in various ways through an appropriate credit policy and by economic policy measures of others kinds.

(3) *Credit policy and the expanding firms*

Credit restrictions have aimed at facilitating borrowing by the preferred sectors—Government and housing—and they have therefore in all probability penalized the non-preferred sectors, i.e. the private sector in general and perhaps industry in particular.[2] Since it must often have seemed desirable to the credit institutions to concentrate on ensuring the future repayment of loans already granted by making new credits available, it may be assumed that in industry the restrictions have operated to some extent at the expense of *new production and new enterprises*.

On the other hand, it has sometimes been argued that the large and efficient enterprises have been able to obtain the necessary capital for expansion. Self-financing has naturally been an important factor here. But it is not difficult to find complaints from this quarter as well about the cumbrous nature of credit restrictions. For example, the large enterprises have been hit by the restrictions on the bond market, and this has at least tended to make their borrowing more expensive. However, it has been argued even more forcibly that small and weak enterprises have suffered continually from the difficulties of raising capital, despite controls and an artificially low level of interest rates. It is perhaps mainly in this last respect that free competition between firms for capital can have a favourable effect. A higher interest

---

[1] See Ulf af Trolle, *Problem inom den tyngre konfektions industrin* (Problems of the Heavy Clothing Industry), Gothenburg, 1961.

[2] See Table on page 69.

charge can be expected to help remove the economically inefficient, less profitable, activity.

The lower level of interest rates, which has been the object of credit market controls, has probably tended to raise the demand for capital. Part of the demand which has in fact emerged would in all likelihood have disappeared as a result of the higher level of interest rates that would have followed from a more liberal credit policy during the years of expansion. At the same time it seems conceivable that a more liberal credit policy during years of stagnation would make possible a lower level of interest rates than would otherwise prevail. This would be an advantage from the employment point of view. In other words, cyclical fluctuations in the level of interest rates would be larger under a liberal credit policy. This should also lead, however, to a higher average level of interest rates over the whole business cycle. Naturally, it is not possible to measure the 'excess demand' for capital that emerged under the fairly low interest rates of the boom, but it presumably came from firms which would have had difficulty in paying a higher price. In this way the shortage of capital has increased, to the detriment of more profitable firms, whom it would have paid to borrow even at (say) 10 per cent, compared with the alternative of making a new issue of shares at perhaps 15 per cent.

The Government has in addition provided direct or indirect subsidies through the budget for the benefit of less profitable types of activity. Ignoring housing for the moment, one example that springs to mind is the increase of about 125 million crowns in farm incomes in the 1960/61 budget year through price control measures. Then there are subsidies to business associations. Local authorities too seem sometimes to have been involved, e.g. through making vacant industrial sites available.[1] These various fiscal subsidies would probably amount to a fairly sizeable total for the whole economy, but nevertheless they are probably less important than the indirect subsidies obtained as a result of the general credit policy that has prevailed.

Credit policy has often been reproached for the way in which the controls have weakened competition between the institutions of the credit market. This is undoubtedly correct, and it has probably meant both less flexibility in lending and higher prices for loans. But perhaps even more important is the fact that competition between borrowers in the market has been reduced by virtue of the fact that the allocation of credit has been determined far too much by controls and far too little by the criterion of profitability. The credit institutions may be guilty of conservatism in their assessments of

[1] This problem is discussed in Chapter X in the section on location policy.

borrowers, but controls can easily lead to an even less rational allocation of credit. Restrictions have probably encouraged a rationing mentality, which favours the allocation of a short supply among as many customers as possible. The obverse of this has been that those who could not have their loan requirements met in the normal way have tried to borrow elsewhere, from suppliers and customers. Where this has succeeded some of the disadvantages of credit restrictions have no doubt been offset.

But such a 'grey' market has disadvantages. It means that credit transactions are linked with ordinary business activity, and this is economically inadvisable. For example, purchases may be made where funds can be borrowed, instead of where goods are cheapest. The borrower's freedom to choose the cheapest and most convenient form of finance is also lost. Clearly, this kind of thing tends to reduce productivity.

Current credit policy has probably served to increase rather than to diminish the built-in resistance of the credit system to change, to damp productivity and progress through helping to tie capital and labour down in less profitable firms.

AN APPRAISAL OF CURRENT CREDIT POLICY

The information about trends in investment and consumption ratios which is given in the following Table sheds some light on the results of recent credit policy, although many other factors have obviously been at work as well.

The Table, and particularly the five-year moving averages in the lower part, shows that total domestic investment has claimed a growing share of the gross national product, and total consumption a correspondingly smaller share. The private investment ratio has remained unchanged, the whole increase in the total investment share having fallen to the public sector. The share of private consumption has fallen most. As is obvious from other sections of this book, we consider that capital formation may have to be increased for a variety of reasons, so that the investment ratio will rise. It will probably tend to do so in any event, even without economic policy consciously operating in this direction. In order to contain the need to increase the investment ratio we consider that selective measures of a different kind from those hitherto employed ought to be used. These should aim at attracting capital to those sectors where it can be expected to give the largest return. This is all the more essential if the private investment ratio should happen to remain unchanged in the long run. If credit policy helps to ensure that some of the less profitable activity is discontinued the need for capital in certain sectors will thereby be reduced.

We have already argued that the need to raise productivity has become much greater as a result of world political developments, the integration of international trade within and outside Europe, and

PUBLIC AND PRIVATE CONSUMPTION AND INVESTMENT

Year	Gross domestic investment as percentage of gross national product[1]			Consumption as percentage of gross national product[1]	
	Private	Public	Total	Private	Total
1938/39	17·5	6·8	24·3	66·2	74·1
1946	18·6	7·8	26·4	63·9	73·6
1950	17·9	9·9	27·8	62·0	72·2
1955	17·3	12·6	29·9	57·2	69·0
1956	17·5	12·7	30·2	56·8	68·7
1957	17·1	13·1	30·2	55·6	67·9
1958	17·9	13·1	31·0	56·8	69·6
1959	17·9	13·7	31·6	55·6	68·7
1960	18·6	13·1	31·8	54·0	66·9
1961	18·7	12·7	31·4	54·1	67·0
1962	18·8	13·0	31·8	53·8	67·3
1963[2]	18·8	13·0	32·3	54·0	67·7
	Five year moving average				
1946–50	18·1	9·0	27·1	63·3	73·3
1947–51	17·9	9·4	27·3	61·9	72·1
1948–52	17·1	10·1	27·2	60·3	70·8
1949–53	17·1	10·9	28·0	59·2	70·0
1950–54	17·4	11·6	29·0	58·5	69·6
1951–55	17·2	12·8	29·4	57·6	68·9
1952–56	17·3	12·7	30·0	57·5	69·2
1953–57	17·4	12·9	30·3	57·1	69·0
1954–58	17·5	12·9	30·4	56·9	69·0
1955–59	17·5	13·0	30·6	56·4	68·8
1956–60	17·8	13·1	31·0	55·8	68·4
1957–61	18·0	13·2	31·2	55·4	68·2
1958–62	18·2	13·1	31·3	55·2	68·2
1959–63[3]	18·2	13·1	31·6	54·6	68·7

Note: The percentages do not always add to 100 because of investment overseas, which is not shown here. Only investment in fixed capital is included. Official Swedish investment statistics include the value of repair and maintenance as well as defence investment and are therefore not fit for international comparisons.

[1] Gross national product at market prices, or total production of goods and services.

[2] Preliminary national budget forecast for 1963.

[3] Part forecast.

the need to help the countries supplying raw materials to industrialize. From this point of view, it is not the question of credit policy versus fiscal policy which is the most important, but of measures in both these areas of policy that promote productivity versus those that do not. Neither must be pursued in such a way as to impede economic progress. From the productivity viewpoint, we consider that a credit policy less hampered by Government controls should be pursued in future, so that scarce capital is better used. This policy does, however, appear to need modification in one important sector, namely housing.

HOUSING POLICY

The consequences of a more liberal credit policy would be particularly important for the provision of capital for house-building, which in some respects occupies a unique position. It is extremely important for the long period that elapses between the planning of a housing scheme and its completion to be given due consideration. Not enough attention has always been paid in recent years to the fact that changes in Government loan terms and conditions must not be made so suddenly that newly-completed projects and work in progress run the risk of becoming superfluous. A surplus or shortage of particular types of residence could very easily arise if there was a sudden switch in demand, so that it no longer coincided with the types of accommodation being produced. For these reasons the housing sector must in our view be insulated against rapid changes in interest rates. Various technical solutions are possible for this problem, which is a quite separate one from the question of subsidizing housing through a permanently *low* rate of interest. As to this latter point, we recommend that a realistic assessment should be made of the likely pattern of interest rates, and the rate of interest applicable to house-building should then be adjusted gradually in accordance with the general movement of interest rates. To continue making loans available at 4 per cent when current interest rates are higher and rising is in fact tantamount to an increase in interest subsidies; Government loans at 4 per cent in fact amount to a long-term subsidy, and not simply a cushion against temporarily high interest rates. Lower subsidies would of course presuppose an increase in the family allowances for housing which are subject to a means test, but a policy of this kind would nevertheless have a positive effect on the Government budget, particularly over the long term.

In general, it seems highly desirable that action should be taken to eliminate the housing shortage more quickly, for unless this is done it is likely to become more severe within the next ten years, both because of the growing numbers of young people and the influx to densely populated areas. The housing shortage militates directly against economic progress if houses cannot be obtained for workers in areas where production could otherwise be increased. More saving by young people is one of many possible ways of easing the finance of house-building which we would like to mention. Measures to stimulate savings may well be justified in this case. In the long run the Pension Funds should also contribute to ensuring adequate finance for house-building.

GOVERNMENT BORROWING

An attempt must be made in future to reconcile productivity and priorities in such a way that productivity receives more attention than it has been given hitherto. Of course the more sectors in addition to house-building that are given priority, the more difficult it becomes to achieve the desired productivity. How large a part of the capital market ought then to be given special treatment? This is a question of the utmost importance. How much regard should then be paid to interest charges on Government borrowing for purposes other than housing?

So far credit policy has been operated in such a way as to reduce the costs of Government borrowing and the need for other contributions. Legislation along the lines proposed by the committee on the credit market could obviously be used in a general way, and not simply at the peak of a boom, to keep down the level of interest rates. In this context the committee stated that it has taken account only of the need to safeguard housing and Government finance, not because these activities would be more important than all others, but because the Government reaches decisions on these questions which must be executed. This seems to us far too formalistic a view of the matter. Confronted as we are with international trade integration it can be said, with greater justification than ever before, that the finance of investment in the *private* sector must be safeguarded. If the central and local governments are prepared to compete with other borrowers for funds they should, since they have the power of taxation, be well able to look after their needs. To grant long-term priorities to public borrowing can almost be said to involve credit policy acting as a support for fiscal policy. It is undoubtedly possible, on the other hand, that rising interest costs may discourage Government borrowing, and in particular lead to the curtailment of local authority activities, which may prove harmful in the long run.

Opinions can clearly differ about how large a part of central and local government borrowing for purposes other than housing would require some priority. We are of the opinion that, in so far as special rules are needed outside the house-building sector, these should perhaps apply to those parts of public activity directly connected with it.[1]

DISTRIBUTIVE ASPECTS OF CREDIT POLICY

In general, we recommend a more liberal credit policy because of the favourable effect it should have on the structure of the economy. But it has been made clear above that this cannot be applied indiscriminately to all sectors of the economy. Even allowing for these modifications, it is worth looking briefly at an additional aspect of a more liberal credit policy. Might it not have consequences for the distribution of income and property in the country which would, on closer examination, make it unacceptable? As is well known, many people hold the view that wage earners lose when interest rates rise, and that they are therefore harmed by a credit policy which leads to higher interest rates.

The Institute of Economic Research has made a quantitative estimate of the immediate effect of the rise in the rate of interest in 1957 on the income and expenditure of households on account of interest. The direct income effect seems to have been negligible and to have reduced rather than increased the inequality in the distribution of income; net outlays were found to increase with rising income. The result would, however, have been very different if the increase in interest rates had led (which it did not) to an immediate general increase in rents. In particular the highest income group in the Institute's material—those who found themselves in the position of having to pay higher interest charges on mortgage loans with variable rates of interest—would then have obtained an increase in incomes as a result of higher rental receipts. On the other hand, the same high income group would have suffered a capital loss if the rise in interest rates had been of a more long-term character, an aspect which the Institute had no cause to take into consideration in its calculations. (Prices of bonds and shares fall when the rate of interest rises.) To the extent that a rise in interest rates forms one part of a long-term policy of reducing the risks of inflation and excess demand, this means that the real return obtained by business firms, or 'the real rate of interest', declines in relation to the money rate of interest.

When all is said and done, there can be few capitalists who have a definite stake even in high long-term rates of interest. They would tend to be the really large savers through the banks, with no debts, and there do not appear to be very many of them about. As in the

[1] Some related points on government business activity are made in Chapter XI.

question of the gains and losses from inflation, it is extremely difficult to tell which groups can be considered to gain and lose by higher rates of interest. Most people in the large social groups of wage earners and business men are just as much lenders as borrowers, and the effect of interest rate changes is then neutralized for these groups as a whole. Obviously this need not be the case for smaller groups of particular individuals. A higher rate of interest, like higher taxes, is both a measure against inflation and an indication of inflation or of a very high level of economic activity. It is one of the prices of full employment, and a price worth paying for the vast majority of the population. Thus distributional considerations should be given very little weight in decisions about future credit policy and interest rates.

PROBLEMS OF SELF-FINANCING

Self-financing by enterprises is another problem which requires brief consideration. The 'natural' conservatism in lending which was discussed above, strengthened by the rigidities of restrictions and rationing, has acted as a stimulus to self-financing. Fiscal policy as well has clearly been an important factor in this trend, which has been simplified particularly through liberal depreciation and valuation rules. It must be stated quite emphatically that self-financing has been carried too far in the Swedish economy, in the sense that it has been so common that even firms that were incapable of expansion in the long run have largely been able to finance their own investment. One objection to such widespread self-financing relates to the income determination aspect. High profits are a strong element in engendering discontent in the wage-determining process. When business profits are obviously large, the strain on the wage policy of solidarity becomes overwhelming, and leads to wage drift, demands for compensation, and distortions in relative wages. If wage policy is successful, in spite of these difficulties, in moderating and co-ordinating wage demands, a situation can develop which occasions the most serious objections to excessive self-financing, namely that the growth in national wealth largely accrues to the owners of business enterprises.

On the other hand, there are numerous indications that financially strong enterprises will be needed in the future as well. Fixed capital is tending to become more important, and this generally gives rise to greater risks of dumping. The growing market constellations and the general trend to more liberal international trade are increasing the pressure of competition and improving the outlook for particular firms. This is a relevant consideration for the increase in trade with the under-developed countries, which involves even greater risks of dumping. In this kind of situation business firms can no longer be given the support of trade measures, but must be capable of absorbing severe blows and riding out a period of temporary dumping, or of transferring their resources gradually to other types of production. General speaking, this applies to large and powerful enterprises operating in several lines and doing a good deal of self-financing.

One outcome of a more liberal credit policy should be that firms with financial surpluses ought to be more willing to make a larger proportion of these funds available to the capital market, for they could then be certain of being able to borrow when they really needed to do so themselves. Some possible partial reforms would also bring some relief. Thus a greater stimulus to savings for the purchase of shares should be helpful, and in general ease the private sector's capital problems. The changeover to the taxation of business profits on a gross basis which is discussed in the next chapter would make share issues easier, for they are made much more expensive by the high profits tax.

What is needed above all, however, is a better co-ordinated economic policy, so that every part of it can contribute to solving the self-financing problems. We ourselves have no objection to vigorous and profitable enterprises being able to finance their own development. This will emerge, for example, in our discussion of company taxation. If this were to be reformed in the way we shall propose it would probably mean greater differentiation as regards the possibilities of self-financing. Larger surpluses in some quarters could then be made available to other sectors, and a more liberal credit policy could help to make this capital available in the market. Lastly, wages policy, if it could be based on a greatly intensified labour market policy, would not have to pay as much attention as it has in the past to a large clump of weak marginal firms. Self-financing would be in less danger of distorting the distribution of income and wealth; but if these were to become more unequal, whether as a result of self-financing or not, it would in our opinion be the job of economic policy to correct this in various ways, and changes in income and property taxation in particular should then be considered.[1] The National Pension and branch funds we have in mind constitute a final factor working against such inequalities.

A MORE RATIONAL ECONOMIC STRUCTURE THROUGH CREDIT MARKET CO-OPERATION

As has been argued above, the less restrictive credit policy which we recommend would probably mean that expanding enterprises and production could obtain capital more readily and perhaps even more

[1] This subject is discussed at greater length in Chapter VII.

cheaply; for example, some part of the expensive share issues that business firms make could in all probability be replaced by cheaper borrowing via bonds. At the same time, and above all, less profitable types of business would eventually have greater difficulty in satisfying their capital requirements. As far as can be judged, the available capital would in this way be better employed than it has been under the current arrangements. The most fundamental requirement of credit policy in the years ahead is that it should provide, in conjunction with tax policy, international trade and other policies, a general framework of economic activity which is calculated to hasten structural change. Systematic decontrol measures should be employed to increase the free flow of capital and abolish existing controls, with their unfavourable structural effects. Obviously, this does not imply a credit market that is completely devoid of any element of rationing. The price of credit, or rate of interest, can never determine by itself whether or not a loan agreement will be concluded, and the credit institutions will inevitably have to 'ration' their lending even in a credit market which is free from official controls. But can a credit market that is more liberal in this sense be expected to solve the particular problems we expect to arise in the economy in the next few years?

GOVERNMENT CO-OPERATION ESSENTIAL

These problems will probably have to be solved by the use of positive, planned measures as well for the purpose of stimulating the active flow of capital. Even in cases of expanding production, where capital problems would by definition be made easier through a more liberal credit market, rapid technological developments, such as the use of atomic energy, may lead to capital requirements that cannot be met through the normal channels used hitherto. In the same way the expanding markets can be expected to require far more capital in future. Our credit system is not constructed for the solution of major international capital problems, but for the financing of relatively small firms in a small domestic market and with only a modest production (so far) for export. A more integrated credit system would help to solve these problems, at least in part. In fact, however, the free movement of capital has been hampered by countries' insisting on retaining some degree of national manoeuvrability in economic policy. The co-ordination of capital movements among The Six is not at all typical. All this suggests to us that the growing capital needs can probably only be met by Government participation, either independently or in conjunction with private capital, or through the budget or Pension Funds.

The granting of credit to non-industrialized countries provides another example of the growing need for co-operation between Government and industry in the field of credit policy. Disregarding pure Government grants for the moment, and thinking primarily of export credits and guarantees, we can see that here too it is the expanding sectors, and especially the exporting capital goods industries, that are affected.[1]

The availability of capital for stagnating sectors is likely to pose even more awkward problems in the future than it does for growing sectors. Government co-operation must be assumed here to an even greater extent. While one would have expected that private capital could be raised to finance co-operation and mergers among a group of firms within a particular branch it has been shown, in an interesting discussion of Branch Rationalization,[2] that it seems in most cases to be very difficult to mobilize large amounts of private capital for this purpose.

As we have argued in Chapters II and III, we anticipate some branches will encounter such great difficulties, particularly as trade expands with countries that are at present under-developed, that measures of this kind will not suffice. One possible alternative to positive rationalization would be to wear out the capital that has been invested in these branches, refrain from further investment and provision for depreciation, and extract any surplus that could be obtained over and above supplementary costs as remuneration. But this would probably be difficult, or even impossible, in practice, because not all the firms in a branch find themselves in the same situation, and the better firms would find it impossible to carry on 'as usual'. If these firms were also to accept the same method competition would perhaps be intensified so that any surplus in excess of supplementary costs would finally disappear, and production would then have to cease. It is quite understandable if the firms in a stagnating branch regard such methods with distaste. But it seems probable, on the other hand, that they do not perceive the real state of affairs in time, but continue investing and writing down capital, individually or in small groups, to the bitter end.

FORMS FOR GOVERNMENT ACTION

A constructive solution of the stagnation problem will probably necessitate official collaboration in various forms. One *essential*

---

[1] Some points about export credits are discussed in Chapter VIII, on *International Trade Policy*.

[2] See Rune Höglund and others, *Branschrationalisering—mening, metoder, möjligheter* (The Purpose, Methods and Prospects of Branch Rationalization). Stockholm, 1958.

condition that must then be insisted upon is that such aid *must not constitute a long-term subsidy* to any sector that obtains assistance. The official forms selected for providing help ought therefore to be chosen with this fundamental postulate in mind, in order to achieve the best possible guarantee against long-term subsidies. Four possibilities seem open in this connection:

(*a*) Special Reconstruction Institutes could be set up to provide appropriate machinery, and here we refer to what is said in the Government textile enquiry about a possible textile credit Institute.[1]

(*b*) The labour market authorities can use their considerable influence. This possibility is discussed below.

(*c*) Government enterprises, and in particular a Government holding company, could take steps to rationalize the structure of a branch. We return to this aspect in Chapter XI.

(*d*) Joint branch rationalization funds could be set up by the parties to collective bargaining. These are examined in Chapter XIII.

THE LABOUR MARKET ADMINISTRATION AS A RATIONALIZER

Any efforts made to rationalize the structure of the economy through the labour market authorities would undoubtedly give rise to pressures in support of 'conservation'. The main task of these authorities in a full employment economy is, however, to act as an intermediary in transferring labour from surplus areas to areas of shortage, and the labour market agency is therefore much less likely to lend its support in subsidizing industries with excess capacity if this involves the retention in them of labour and other resources. From the trade union point of view, the most essential feature must be to ensure that the workers are given due consideration and that those firms and sectors which are in a position to offer their employees the best working conditions are not denied the opportunity to expand. In general, we would maintain that it is an essential requirement of more rapid structural change, with its accompanying increase in welfare, that both business men and employees should be able to feel certain of obtaining a livelihood, even if it means abandoning their former activity. A strong labour market policy would mean that structural rationalization could correspondingly be pursued at a more rapid rate in branches where excess capacity existed. There need be no doubt about the ability of the labour market agencies as such to make a significant contribution or of its justification on purely objective grounds. The problem is more one of

[1] S.O.U. 1959:42, *Konkurrens under samverkan* (Competition and Co-operation), p. 37 et seq.

administration and administrative law, to which we return below.

If one wishes to go beyond the fairly 'traditional' type of labour market policy discussed in Chapter X it becomes necessary to think in terms of official loans or direct contributions. In the last resort it is only through direct financial contributions to business firms that guarantees can be given against layoffs or the closing down of enterprises at a time which is unfavourable from the point of view of labour market policy. These ought of course only to be used temporarily, as a way of gaining time so that the labour can be given alternative employment at a later date, and they should not be used to provide permanent support for weak firms. Direct contributions could be discontinued when the economic situation improved, and if firms were then unable to maintain their activity they would have to close down, according as the labour force could be placed elsewhere.

Even if this could be done without unemployment being created, it would of course be better if preventive measures could be taken in good time. For example, temporary direct contributions to help production could be linked with the condition that a firm discontinued part of its range of products and concentrated on other parts instead. In such cases it is important for the labour market authorities to be able to act as an intermediary for, or make available, technical assistance so that firms can take up new and more profitable lines of production. The investment required could where necessary be financed in whole or part through official credit guarantees on the authorization of the National Labour Market Board. Co-operation with various credit institutions should be developed with this in view, and it may be necessary to think of some Government fund, coming directly under the Board, for this purpose. The trouble with all this, however, is that it would give the Labour Market Board a position of power which far exceeded that customary for an official agency. Collaboration between the credit institutions, business firms, and the Government must therefore be arranged along other lines. We consider that an appropriate solution could be found in the establishment of a Department of Industry and Employment.

A DEPARTMENT OF INDUSTRY AND EMPLOYMENT

We can safely assume that there will be major investment and credit problems in the economy in the future, and it is therefore extremely important that some permanent form of co-operation should be developed on structural policy between the authorities and the credit institutions. The traditional contacts between the Riksbank and these institutions may make it seem the natural official representative on this question. But there are arguments against this. Consultation between the Riksbank and the institutions has hitherto concerned anti-cyclical questions, and it is in these matters that the Riksbank possesses considerable expertise, e.g. through its international contacts. But the importance of structural questions and the possibility that investigations will be conducted through Departments seem to make the Riksbank an inappropriate choice, and suggest that the co-operation ought instead to take place at Government level. In addition, the National Pension Funds, which will probably play an important part in future questions of finance, ought to be placed on the same organizational footing as other credit institutions.

We propose instead that a Department of Industry and Employment should be established. This would be responsible for dealing with the credit and investment aspects of structural rationalization, as well as acting as the main planning agency in the economy and co-ordinator of Government business enterprises. The head of the Department ought therefore to be responsible for consultation about structural questions between the authorities and the institutions of the credit market, and have an investment council working along with him. In this way the Minister responsible for the department would have all structural questions under his direction. The investment council should include Government representatives, and representatives of the credit market, including the Riksbank and Pension Funds, and of industry and the labour market organizations. Particular branches ought not on the other hand to be represented, but would instead be called in for consultation when the problems of a particular branch were under discussion.

This council, which would be advisory in character, would deal with questions of principle about the structure of the economy, and have power to commission investigations. The Department ought therefore to be equipped with a qualified secretariat for this purpose. Questions of detail and the practical aspects of investment and credit could more appropriately be dealt with through the labour market authorities rather than this investment council.[1]

---

[1] Since this was written, questions concerning the labour market have been placed under the Ministry of the Interior, which now closely resembles the Department of Industry and Employment discussed above. The heads of the Ministries of Finance, Commerce and the Interior now form a board of long range economic planning within the government. They are assisted by a consultative body of 17 representatives from various organizations and research institutions. They have the assistance of the expanded economic department of the Ministry of Finance, which is to issue continually revised long term forecasts.

CHAPTER VII

TAX POLICY

Direct and indirect taxes plus social security payments amounted in the tax year 1960 to over 17,000 millions crowns. The published estimates of the General Committee on Taxation indicate that physical persons were responsible for about 85 per cent and companies for about 15 per cent of this total.

The proportions of total taxation derived from various forms of taxes have fluctuated, partly as a result of cyclical changes in income, for example the shifts in income associated with the Korea inflation, and partly through changes in the forms of taxation themselves, for example the introduction of the General Turnover Tax in 1960. Broadly speaking, the total tax collected from judicial persons (companies and economic associations) has remained unchanged since 1955, but in the same period taxes on physical persons have increased by approximately one-third. Since there has been no visible shift in this period in the gross income share of GNP of both groups, despite quite marked business fluctuations, the explanation seems to lie in the way in which the Swedish tax system itself has operated in favour of business enterprises. Their powers of regulating profits in various ways do not seem to have been noticeably reduced. At the same time the rise in incomes has led to an automatic increase in the progressiveness of the tax system for physical persons, and in addition the yield from social welfare contributions and the indirect taxes which affect private consumption has increased. There have also been increases in local authority taxes.

Taxes can be discussed on the basis of one of two broad divisions: the subjects that pay the different taxes, and the objects (income, property, goods) on which the taxes are imposed. The main classification chosen here is first to discuss the taxation of physical persons, and then company taxation, while the possibility of some redistribution between these two types of taxes is treated as an intermediate feature. Finally, we discuss the possibilities of improving the coordination of the anti-cyclical and stabilization uses of tax policy with its structural aspects.

What should be the tasks of tax policy from a structural point of view? There are two answers to this question:

(1) It should promote the allocation of economic resources in such a way that the major social needs and the important 'basic

investments', which are the responsibility of the public sector, do not tend continually to lag behind, as they have in the past. This allocation is not of course a task for tax policy alone, but the structure of the tax system is one significant aspect of it.

(2) Within the field of private enterprise it should promote, or at any rate not discourage, the highly productive and expanding enterprises. This means, conversely, that tax policy should refrain from tying resources down in low productive, inefficient firms by granting them special tax concessions.

An important requirement here is that it should be possible to achieve these tax objectives without an increase in the inequality of incomes and in the distribution of property. The object should, on the contrary, be to bring about further equalization. If, in fulfilling these structural requirements, tax policy in some respects 'leads us astray' this should be corrected by social policy and through other parts of tax policy, for example, higher estate duties as a corrective against any increase in the concentration of property.

TAXATION OF PHYSICAL PERSONS

In the case of the taxation of individuals, the significance of tax policy for economic progress has often been discussed by reference to such general criteria as the effect of taxation on personal savings and on the incentive to work. It has been argued by the Conservative and Liberal Parties that a relatively high pressure of taxation which aims at taking a large slice of high incomes hampers economic growth.

Let us first examine the assertion about personal savings. It is by no means certain how far this may have been hampered by tax policy. The strong propensity to consume which is typical of the modern welfare society probably means that it is difficult in any circumstances to bring about a noticeable long-term increase in personal savings by means of tax changes. Tax cuts for this purpose would be abortive or far too ineffective. In addition, even if there may be other reasons for encouraging personal saving, such as saving for life assurance purposes, which may be justified for social reasons, the increased saving that is desirable for structural purposes should take place in other forms, e.g. through increased self-financing by the public sector, the capital formation of co-operative enterprises, and savings out of profits by expanding firms. Two important points to bear in mind are that these other forms of saving can be adjusted more readily with fluctuations in business activity, and a very large increase in personal savings means a corresponding cut in consumption, which could have a deflationary effect in certain economic situations. Thus the investment for which the increase in personal saving provided scope would probably not be undertaken on any scale, whereas an increase in Government saving can be matched in quite a different way to the desired volume of investment.

Criticism of the effects of the existing tax system on incentives to work also seem to us to fall wide of the mark. It seems most unlikely that marginal tax rates could in general be responsible for people refraining from work or reducing the amount of work they do. There may be a few cases of this sort, although they are difficult to distinguish from cases of people who, when they wish to restrict their input of labour services, blame taxation for the sake of having something to blame. But it seems unreasonable to argue that taxes would have a restrictive effect in very many cases, or that these would not be more than offset by people who, because of the marginal rate of tax, considered themselves obliged to increase their efforts in order to attain a certain net income target. It must be remembered that for large groups gross incomes have been affected by taxes. In income groups where marginal rates of tax have begun to be relatively high, wage-fixing has helped to provide compensation, and the equalizing effect of progressiveness, which would provide a disincentive, has thus been lessened. One reason for this has been the system of equal percentage increase in wages, which has sometimes maintained or even increased the absolute difference in net wages between different groups. At all events, the possible influence of taxes on the incentive to work of the individual must be insignificant for the total input of labour services in society, compared with an infinitesimally small variation in the total volume of employment caused by fluctuations in business activity.

By these rejoinders to criticisms of the existing system of taxation of physical persons we do not mean to suggest that we consider this system to be well devised in every respect from the structural policy point of view. Although this is not the place to enter into a detailed discussion of the technical aspects of the future structure of this tax, some general observations ought to be made.

If tax policy is to have a favourable effect on the structure of the economy it must ensure that there is a sufficient volume of savings in an expanding economy for purposes of stabilization and for financing a growing public sector within such a economy. This requires that the majority of the population do not consider the taxes to be too severe from a psychological point of view, or interpret them as being directed against the incomes of private individuals. Such a feeling, whether it is justified or not, makes it more difficult politically to levy sufficient taxes. It can readily lead to tax evasion through direct cheating and through the growth of hidden benefits. The latter give rise to tax injustices which are not acceptable from a social point of view, since a privately organized system of adjustment develops alongside that intended through the tax system.

We wish to emphasize strongly that a great deal more can and ought to be done to end this serious state of affairs, through greater controls over tax evasion and changes in the regulations regarding tax avoidance. However, the whole problem of an adequate long-term tax revenue can certainly not be solved in this way, although changes in tax forms which made the control of tax evasion easier would of course be an advantage.

The route that has been explored in Sweden is that of the general turnover tax, i.e. an increase in the burden of indirect taxation, since the direct income tax has been considered too high to permit further increases. The avowed intention is to go further in the same direction, in order to make possible a reduction in the progressiveness of income tax in the lower and medium ranges, and to simplify the structure of direct taxation.[1] The equalizing effect of progressive taxation, which in itself is a structural task, would then largely be taken over by the 'second part' of equalization policy, social policy compensations.

We are sympathetic to the view that taxation should be made more politically manageable, and to the efforts to reduce the progressiveness for income earners in the moderate ranges of incomes and simplify the system, in both cases in conjunction with stronger social policy measures to promote equality.

From the point of view of structural policy it is questionable whether large increases in indirect taxation which impinge directly upon the consumption of the private individual are appropriate. Any drastic increases in this type of tax would run the risk of restricting consumption so much that an important inducement to investment and to economic expansion would disappear; or, alternatively, that taxation would accentuate the decline in the value of money through compensating increases in income being obtained via wage bargaining. Apart from increases in indirect taxes on physical persons which might be justified for particular reasons, e.g. on motor cars, so that they carried a greater share of the costs and brought about a more equitable comparison between different transport costs, or on alcohol, we are doubtful about the wisdom of shifting the total burden of taxes very much further in the direction of taxes on consumption.

One possibility which we think ought to be considered is a redistribution of taxation between physical persons and business firms,

[1] From 1962 there has in fact been a general reduction in progressiveness, and the turnover tax percentage has also been increased.

a suggestion which is also justified by the shift in tax burdens which has occurred to the disadvantage of physical persons. The future place of social security contributions in the tax system is of primary importance in this connection. It may be worth considering whether the costs of social insurance proper could not be financed largely along the lines of the National Pension Scheme, i.e. through removing them entirely or in part from personal income tax and changing over to employer contributions. It seems clear in any event that the impending increase in the co-ordination of the Pension Funds and the old age pension will make such an arrangement a natural one for financing the old age pension. This solution may also have a great deal to be said for it in the case of health insurance, in the light of the changes suggested for this branch of social insurance.

Three points seem particularly important regarding such a possible reconstruction. Firstly, there could be important advantages for personal taxation. There would be a movement away from the existing system, with its progressive scale against which rising personal social security contributions are deductible, and which thus operates regressively. This cannot be considered a rational system either from the point of view of equity or of a flexible tax system. There could be a considerable reduction in the amount of tax payable through the personal income return, depending on how large a part of the cost of social insurance was paid by employers. It would provide scope for a desirable pruning of progressiveness in the lower and medium income tax ranges. Lastly, these changes could avoid the need for major increases in the turnover tax.

Secondly, it should be stated that the ultimate distributive effect is of course not completely clear. A change of this kind in the relative shares of the tax burden between individuals and business firms would be sure to influence employers' arguments in wage negotiations. If, *ceteris paribus*, gross wages were to remain unchanged wage earners would obtain a significant gain in net wages. The outcome would almost certainly depend largely on the wage bargaining situation when the change was made, and of course on its magnitude.

Thirdly, it is clear that the arrangement, in precisely the same way as the National Pension Scheme, would operate as a wage tax upon enterprises. The significant thing from the structural point of view is not so much the total burden as its relative weight for firms with differing proportions of labour inputs. As in the case of the pension scheme, the arrangement would fall more heavily on labour-intensive firms, such as processing and service enterprises. Although these differences between different types of enterprise must not be exaggerated, the structural effect would involve pressure to rationalize in the labour-intensive parts of enterprise. The alternative method of financing, an increase in the general turnover tax in association with a reconstructed direct tax system, would not be likely to exercise the same pressure. Naturally, it would be necessary to ensure that such a reform did not operate too severely against labour-intensive enterprises, particularly through its sudden introduction. Both the final amount of the costs of social insurance that can appropriately be transferred and the rate at which this should take place must be clarified before any final decision is made.

COMPANY TAXATION

The idea that business firms ought to carry a larger share of the costs of social insurance in the form of direct dues harmonizes well with our view that company taxation should be completely reconstructed for structural reasons.

If we begin by looking at the existing system of company taxation, it is often urged, particularly by industry, that in general this tax seriously impedes self-finance and consolidation by business firms. These assertions do not seem to be correct. As a matter of fact, taxes account on the average for only a small percentage of the total outlays of those companies which pay any profits tax at all.[1]

The decisive part which taxation is often said to play in the finance of business firms thus gives an exaggerated impression of its significance. The probable explanation for exaggerating its influence is that taxation is interpreted as the 'unnecessary' cost operating at the margin. It is true that some modifications have been made to the free right of depreciation which was introduced in the reform of 1947, but new opportunities have nevertheless been provided for obtaining significant advantages in tax assessments. Thus the right to allocate funds to investment reserves[2] gives business firms a considerable tax concession. The various opportunities which have been available to business firms for regulating profits by way of the allocations they make have in total meant that business firms have largely paid an unchanged amount of tax in recent years, despite the rising trend of profits before making provision for depreciation and allocations to investment reserves. The level of self-financing in industry has also been high.

Other objections have, however, been made to the existing system

[1] For example, tax paid as a percentage of gross receipts in 1958 averaged 4·3 per cent for all enterprises, and ranged from 0·8 per cent in the textile and clothing industry to 7·3 per cent for hydro-electric power stations.

[2] This arrangement allows a company to set aside part of its profits as an investment reserve (investeringsfond) which then enjoys favourable tax treatment. The intention is that the reserves should be used for counter-cyclical purposes, with the permission of the National Labour Market Board.

of company taxation which we regard as much more significant. They can be summarized in the following three points:

(1) The effect on productivity of the present form of company taxation is clearly harmful in certain respects. It encourages firms to develop a 'tax mentality', which leads to the allocation of resources that is justified by tax considerations but which is irrational on a broader economic view. The very attitude that 'the Government pays half the cost' militates against the careful screening of projects, and leads to a waste of resources which is noticeable, for example, with regard to office equipment, business representation, and the salaries of senior executives. The valuation and control problems in the administration of the tax on net profits also make it a fairly laborious system to operate, both for the authorities and business firms.

(2) It is more difficult to determine the general effects of the tax on net profits and to discover, for example, which types of enterprise it favours and which it penalizes. This of course is its most important effect, and the one that ought to be decisive in determining the structure of the tax. However, if the existing burden of taxation on enterprises as shown by profits statistics is compared against 'gross receipts' or 'manufacturing, selling and administrative costs' for different years, a very clear tendency emerges. Present company taxation is a greater burden on firms with low costs in relation to gross receipts than on others. In general, profits tax operates in such a way that, on the average, industrial firms are most highly taxed and, within industry, it is the export firms that are hardest hit. From the structural point of view, therefore, the existing tax has the effect of burdening the large enterprises, particularly export firms, and industry as a whole.

Whether or not this effect is considered discriminatory depends of course on the point of view from which the matter is judged. It is often argued that the taxation of net profits is 'equitable'. It allocates the tax according to ability-to-pay, by which is meant the amount of the net profit. In our view this parallel with the income tax on physical persons is largely irrelevant, quite apart from the false impression of objectiveness attaching to the ability-to-pay principle in this context. In any case the achievement of such equity is not the intention of the taxation of net profits, but rather an indication that it has missed its mark. Moreover, the job of company taxation must first and last be to promote the long-term evolution of the economy towards higher productivity and growth. Arguments about equity and justice must come later, for example through a capital gains tax and higher inheritance taxes on the owners of business firms.

(3) Taken along with the characteristics of the net profits tax system discussed above, this point makes it clear that the system to

some extent creates, or at least preserves, an allocation of investment and other resources which is unfavourable from the point of view of structural policy. In fact it operates as a subsidy to less profitable firms, which obtain an equalizing item on the cost side through their comparatively low tax burden, or even escape the tax altogether, as is the case with the majority of small companies. The effect is to reduce the movement of factors of production from less to more rational enterprises. In short, it increases the very rigidities in the economy which, on the thesis of this book, we are striving to eliminate.

It can naturally be argued that this rigidity is offset to some extent by tax incidence. Taxes would be shifted so that the consumer would still pay them in the end. Even if we assume that this shifting occurs in the case of the net profits tax as well as other taxes it does not eliminate the importance of the form of the tax for productivity. (In any case, the behaviour of business firms in practice suggests that the differences assumed in theory with regard to the shifting of different business taxes to prices or wages are certainly exaggerated.) If the tax is shifted this is expressed in higher prices, and the firms paying the highest taxes would then be exposed to the pressure of fixing unnecessarily high prices for their products, thereby reducing their competitiveness and hampering their growth prospects. Tax increases, either via a higher percentage rate and/or levies on investment, which are undertaken for anti-cyclical purposes accentuate the progressiveness of company taxation, and the tax system, which in itself is unfavourable from the point of view of structural policy, is made additionally unfavourable. Conversely, the effect is mitigated when such extra impositions are removed.

Various objections have been raised to a complete or partial changeover from the taxation of net profits to some form of taxation of business enterprises on a gross basis. It may be sufficient to mention the most important of these.

(1) It has been argued that the starting-point for this criticism is itself erroneous, in that the alleged progressive effect of the taxation of net profits is said to be greatly exaggerated. This objection does not seem to have been supported by the detailed investigations made so far.

(2) Gross taxation has been said to give rise to major difficulties for firms conducted in the form of partnerships, which would be taxed both as enterprises and through the taxation of the owners as physical persons. This is of course in itself a correct statement. But in our view it does not constitute a serious objection to the gross form of taxation. A business partnership is in the same situation as public companies of the same size; what is taken in the form of gross

taxes is deducted from the profit remaining for the owners, precisely as any other cost of production, and there is no double taxation of the owner as an income recipient. If an excess burden arises from the total tax point of view, and in certain cases this will undoubtedly be the result, this is not because the new system is erroneous but because the old system gives these firms far too favoured a position which, on structural grounds, is unduly conservative from the point of view of the movement towards larger units of production.

(3) It has been argued that gross taxation would be particularly irksome for export firms. The idea is that, while no one could shift a tax on net profits to any great extent, this could happen in the home market in the case of the gross form of taxation. Export firms, on the other hand, which are dependent on the prices fixed in foreign markets, would not be able to shift it and their position would be worsened, relatively speaking. Apart from the fact that the difference in the possibilities of shifting the taxes is probably not very great as between the two forms of tax (if, indeed, there is any at all in the short run), the argument appears untenable in view of the expectation that our export markets will continue to expand. Export firms would probably face no special difficulties of shifting compared with other firms, and in any case the gross tax would represent a very small part of total costs.

(4) The completely opposite argument has also been put, namely that export firms would shift a gross tax by raising their prices, and this tax would then be included in the price on which the consuming country was imposing its indirect taxes, including customs duties. This could be a source of irritation and be interpreted as contrary to the provision of GATT.[1] But it is difficult to understand how there could be any difference from the point of view of the consuming country between the price of an export good being raised through a tax on the net profits of the export firms and its being raised by the taxation of gross receipts in the producing country. It does not seem reasonable to regard a general gross tax which replaces a tax on net profits, either in whole or in part, as in any way discriminatory against the purchasers of exports.

(5) Finally, it has been argued that the type of company taxation adopted is of secondary importance from the structural point of view compared, for example, with a generally restrictive economic policy, which would bring to an end the 'subsidizing' of the less efficient enterprises through inflation. This argument seems to be completely beside the point. The fact that such an economic policy may in itself

1 The General Agreement on Tariffs and Trade, which was concluded in 1947 under the auspices of the United Nations, is intended to promote the abolition of tariffs and the removal of other obstacles to trade.

be important structurally, and perhaps be more important than the form of company taxation, does not prevent the form of company taxation, in conjunction with economic policies that are more or less restrictive in other respects, from playing an extremely important part in structural change.

Our conclusion is that it seems more appropriate on general grounds of structural policy to adopt a gross form of tax than to abide by the existing net profits tax; the most serious objections raised against taxation on a gross basis do not seem to be so overwhelming as to act as a deterrent. Of course this is not to deny that other and more serious objections may appear on closer investigation. In particular, there may be some uncertainty about how thorough the reconstruction ought to be, whether, for example, the gross form of tax should be adopted entirely or only in part, and whether it should form the major or only a small proportion of the total taxation of business enterprise.

The examination which is being made by the general tax enquiry into the various possible forms that gross taxation might take, e.g. a tax imposed on gross expenditure, on the utilization of raw materials alone, or on transformation values (a tax on surplus value), should provide a lead which is lacking at present. It should also be emphasized that any changeover ought to take place by easy stages, so that business firms do not have to face too drastic adjustments.

A more comprehensive changeover to the gross form of taxation would obviously influence the allocations which business firms make at present with a view to regulating profits. The present investment reserves would thus have to be reviewed, for this type of counter-cyclical measure would no longer seem as 'natural'. Exemption from, or postponement of, taxation under such arrangements could no longer be practised in the same way, since there would then be no profits tax on which to base deductions. In principle a corresponding right of deduction could be allowed under the gross tax system. But it would probably be rather complicated, and it would almost certainly be more appropriate to operate changes in company taxation for anti-cyclical and stabilization purposes by means of changes in the percentage rate of the gross tax levied on companies, which in itself would probably be a more flexible weapon for regulating profits than the existing measures. If the gross and net profits tax were to be combined, then both the 'old' and the 'new' methods could of course be used, either independently or in conjunction.

SHORT- AND LONG-RUN TAX PERSPECTIVES

Finally, something should be said from the structural point of view about the anti-cyclical and stabilization uses of taxation. Such measures also have important structural effects, whether the changes in tax yields operate rather blindly, through the deficits and surpluses that occur automatically as a result of shifts in incomes in the course of business fluctuations, or more consciously, and in a more differentiated way, through direct variations in the tax yield and in the distribution of taxes among different subjects and objects. Whatever the initial structure of the tax system, therefore, it is important that tax changes which are made for stabilization purposes should be looked at in the context of the structural objectives. When, for example, some stimulus against stagnation has to be provided, it may be necessary to choose between tax reductions that would increase demand in the private sector and increases in public expenditure with an unchanged tax burden. Any decisions should be taken against the background of the long-run objectives for the public and private sectors respectively. Increases in expenditure rather than tax cuts are then preferable from the structural viewpoint if there are shortcomings and neglected projects in the public sector. Conversely, when restrictive measures become necessary, the same objective should be pursued via tax increases in preference to expenditure cuts in the public sector. Despite the awareness of the needs of structural growth in this sector, it is not a systematic policy which calls, as has regularly happened, for restrictions on investment and halts to expenditure in the public sector.

In this sort of situation tax increases ought accordingly to be allocated in different ways according to the objectives. If, as we consider is appropriate, one wished to stimulate the expanding sectors of enterprise, tax increases should not for example be imposed on these sectors which the less efficient firms would feel only slightly, if at all. This was to some extent the case with the investment levy[1] (from which small firms were exempt) and the extra company tax (by which 'unprofitable' firms were not in fact affected).

Stabilization needs may of course clash with structural requirements in certain situations. The economy may be so overstrained that all the brakes have to be applied at once in order to prevent excess demand and inflation. 'Good' investments are then affected along with the 'less good', rapidly expanding firms with those which are in structural decline. But this must be regarded as exceptional.

The objective must as far as possible be to dovetail stabilizing tax measures and structural objectives in such a way that the long-term view is never overlooked. We are aware that this may impose a severe political strain, especially when there is a sharp downturn for

[1] This was a tax levied in 1951–52 and 1955–57 in the form of a gross percentage tax on investment above a certain minimum.

particular branches and firms. It may often seem much simpler to give way to demands for tax cuts (or other subsidies) for firms that suffer.

An assumption underlying our whole argument here is of course the active labour market policy described in Chapter X. One of the advantages of such a policy is precisely that it provides greater possibilities for pursuing a stabilizing tax policy which is more consciously geared to structural requirements.

CHAPTER VIII

INTERNATIONAL TRADE POLICY

International trade policy has always been a prominent weapon in the arsenal of economic policy, although it has undergone or is in the process of undergoing a fundamental change. In the inter-war years foreign trade policy involved the export of unemployment through protectionist devices, but in the post-war period of full employment it has been directed, at least in principle, to the liberalization of world trade. Whether recent integration policy is regarded as part of this process, or purely as power politics, it is evident both that foreign trade policy is of fundamental importance and that it has now acquired new and more structural tasks. At the same time, some parts of the former policy, such as the significance of customs duties for the Government budget, now seem less prominent than they were.

The advantages of international division of labour, which have long been recognized in principle, form the background to the 'new' foreign trade policy. Just as modern society, in contrast to previous self-sufficient economies, is based on the assumption that individuals exchange their produce with one another, so ought this also to apply in principle to countries. If every good were to be produced by every country, production would in many cases need to take place on such a small scale that it took the form of handicraft, high cost, production. Each country ought instead to concentrate on those activities for which it has the best natural endowment, in the sense of raw materials, capital, and also skilled labour. Even where good natural conditions favour a wide variety of productive activities the small countries in particular should nevertheless concentrate on fewer sectors in order to avoid excessive dispersion of their resources. If each country concentrates its manufacturing activity on those sectors in which it can hold its own most effectively in international trade this in the first instance promotes efficiency and increases competition. Unprofitable and unproductive firms find it increasingly difficult to maintain their position in the market, and this hastens the rationalization of the structure of the economy. If industry is expanded with this object in view, international division of labour will in time be increasingly achieved, and every increase in international trade will bring greater welfare and a better utilization of the world's productive resources.

With this general principle in mind we shall proceed to discuss protectionist arguments in greater detail after we have examined recent Swedish trade policy. Thereafter we shall consider how far European integration and relations with the under-developed countries can provide justification for a departure from the principle of free trade, and the final section will be devoted to a discussion of the relationship between foreign trade policy and other parts of economic policy.

(1) *Trends in the average level of tariffs*

The simplest way of measuring the level of tariffs is to take the receipts from customs duties as a percentage of total imports in the same year. Since a number of goods, particularly raw materials, are exempt from customs duties and these account for almost half total imports into Sweden, a clearer picture of the level of tariffs and protection is obtained by looking instead at customs receipts in relation to imports of dutiable commodities alone. This gives a figure of 10·8 per cent for the year 1959, which means that Swedish customs duties amounted on average to about 11 per cent of the value of the goods at the ports of entry before customs duties were imposed. Thus customs duties are considerably higher if they are measured in relation to foreign export prices (f.o.b.). The following table shows the post-war trend of Swedish tariffs:

			Level of tariffs (percentages)	
			All goods	Dutiable goods
1946	..	..	6·5	11·5
1947	..	..	6·4	10·5
1948	..	..	5·4	10·1
1949	..	..	5·2	10·1
1950	..	..	5·2	9·4
1951	..	..	4·3	8·0
1952	..	..	4·4	8·0
1953	..	..	5·2	8·2
1954	..	..	5·5	8·9
1955	..	..	5·6	8·9
1956	..	..	5·4	9·5
1957	..	..	5·3	9·3
1958	..	..	6·0	9·7
1959	..	..	6·2	10·8
1960	..	..	6·0	—
1961	..	..	6·1	—

Whichever of these measures of tariffs is used there was, at least relatively, a fairly clear reduction up to 1951, and from 1953 an

93

increase approximately as large. The reduction in the period 1946–51 had a particular explanation. At that time Swedish customs duties were mainly specific duties, i.e. a certain amount of money was paid per unit of the commodity, per kilo etc. When import prices rose during these years, while the rate of customs duty remained unchanged, the customs duty levied in relation to the value of the goods therefore declined. The level of tariffs fell. In the period 1952–54 the opposite occurred.

The continued rise in the level of customs duties from 1955 has, on the other hand, been the result of a deliberate policy. In the summer of 1955 customs duties, particularly on textiles but also on other consumer goods, were raised provisionally, in broad agreement with the proposals of the Committee on Tariffs.[1] These proposals only came before the Riksdag (Parliament) in their entirety in 1958, and after some minor adjustments a new tariff schedule came into operation in 1959 which led to a new increase in the level of tariffs. In addition there was at about the same time a further upward adjustment through the introduction of minimum weight tariffs on certain consumer goods, in addition to those that existed in the *new* customs tariff which had already been decided upon. In contrast to the old system, the new system contains *ad valorem* duties, i.e. the customs duty is a proportion, e.g. 10 per cent, of the value of the goods brought in. Duties of this type were now combined in certain cases with provisions of the type 'but a minimum of 4 crowns per kilo'. Since *ad valorem* duties give a fairly low customs revenue on cheap goods, a minimum sum duty can in these cases mean a further considerable rise in customs duties, and this is what happened.

The table shows there was a tendency for the level of customs duties to fall during 1960, in connection with the first tariff reductions among the countries of The Seven; but this has been offset in part as a result of the previous tariff schedule decisions, which have gradually affected the amount and composition of imports.

It can be argued that the increase in tariffs during the period 1950–60 was in fact more significant than the statistics show. If import prices rise while specific customs duties remain unchanged, this means that the level of tariffs declines, as occurred up to the year 1952. But the changeover to *ad valorem* duties in the new customs schedules cut short this tendency for tariffs to be reduced automatically in a full employment society. This changeover in fact was thus equivalent to a failure to reduce tariffs.

These figures perhaps fail to tell the whole story in other respects as well. Apart from direct increases in tariffs, the level of tariffs may conceivably rise through an increase in the import of precisely those

[1] *Tulltaxa. Förslag av 1952 års tulltaxekommitté.* S.O.U. 1956: 14–16.

goods on which comparatively high tariffs are levied. It would then be necessary, as has sometimes been argued, to study the changes in tariffs on different groups of goods before the reasons behind the rise in tariffs mentioned could be clarified. Against this, there have undoubtedly been some direct tariff increases, and in addition the main idea underlying the tariff revision was precisely that of using tariffs in the most protective way, namely to reduce or abolish them in sectors where they were least required (where imports were unimportant), and to increase them where imports and the need for protection were greatest. The result has inevitably been to increase the average level of tariffs.

(2) *The level of tariffs for different goods*

An examination of different goods indicates the correctness of what has been said, and it also provides a starting-point for assessing how tariff increases ought to be adjusted from the resource use point of view. Which parts of the economy have benefited and which have lost by it? It may be useful in this context to go back to the calculations which the Committee on Tariffs once made of the level of tariffs on various groups of goods. We are primarily interested here in the changes, and therefore we shall ignore the absolute level of tariffs. If the level of tariffs on imports in 1950 according to the customs rates then in force is compared with the level of tariffs which would have followed if the Committee's proposals had been adopted, we find that the largest percentage increases in customs duties would have been recorded for the following groups of goods: knitted woollen, cotton, and rayon goods and woven goods of materials other than artificial silk; leather and skins; wooden furniture; and, to a lesser extent, porcelain goods, iron and metal manufactures, and inorganic chemical products in general. On the other hand, the most significant reductions in tariffs would, according to the committee's calculations, have occurred for woven goods of artificial silk and leather footwear. In addition, this last category had its net customs protection reduced through the higher tariff on the raw materials, leather and skins, and similarly the higher duties on ready-made clothing were largely neutralized through higher tariffs on most textiles. For other groups of industries the Committee's proposals were not considered to involve any major changes in the level of tariffs on imports. All that need be added is that the Committee's proposals were very largely put into force, the deviations tending rather to accentuate these changes, and that this was also the purport of the minimum tariffs introduced in 1958.

Before we proceed further, let us interpose a few words about foodstuffs. Here customs duties on the most important products are replaced by import levies, to make it administratively possible to change them more rapidly, to avoid accounting for the resulting revenues in the Government budget, and in order to use them for regulatory purposes. In addition to this, domestic production and consumption are subject to certain duties in order to collect the resources for subsidizing the export of surplus agriculture production. Compared with other raw materials and fuels, which either have no or very small customs duties, the import protection for foodstuffs is thus very high, ranging from 20 per cent to over 80 per cent of the import value, and averaging about 45 per cent.

This method of supplementing tariff protection with import controls also applies to some industrial products which have comparatively high duties. During the past ten years import quotas have been practically abolished in our trade with other Western European countries, and recently for imports from the USA and other areas as well. But they are still used as a protective device against imports from Eastern Europe.

Against all this it can naturally be argued that the Swedish tariff level is nevertheless very low by international standards, that our trading policy is comparatively liberal in other respects, and also that we have, through the reduction in customs duties in the EFTA countries since 1960, again acquired a somewhat lower average level of customs duties. This trend is likely to gather additional momentum in the future as well. These objections are undoubtedly correct, but nonetheless they do not blunt the criticism made here. If the Government considered it was advantageous for Sweden to be a low tariff country, why has the level of tariffs been raised? If on the other hand it is argued that the tariff increases are advantageous and necessary, because other countries have a greater measure of protection for their economies, this is calculated to arouse misgivings that attempts will continue to be made to raise our customs duties, or that our foreign trade policy will be tightened up wherever this is still possible. That such attempts are made is unfortunately undeniable.

ARGUMENTS FOR PROTECTION UNTENABLE

(1) *The employment and economic situation argument*

The general employment situation has provided no justification for an increase in long-term tariff protection, for it has been difficult to obtain work on only two occasions in the post-war years, the winters of 1952–53 and 1958–59, whereas periods of labour shortage have been much more enduring. In our view, the fundamental point is that the tariff level has been raised during a marked period of boom, at a time when labour has been scarce in the expanding sectors and a great need has existed for re-training and re-allocating employees and re-arranging the location of the stock of enterprises. The opportunities for transferring people have never been better than they are at the present time. Swedish tariffs may be low by international standards, but we must not content ourselves with that. It is most regrettable that even a moderate raising of tariffs should have occurred in such favourable economic conditions, and that the whole trend of Swedish tariff policy has been misconceived.

A policy of this kind, applied during boom years when labour and capital were very scarce, must have tended to conserve the structure of the economy, and Sweden has in all probability been saddled with more old, unprofitable, low wage types of activity than would otherwise have been the case, and in our having been less able to develop the rapidly expanding and profitable branches with high wage levels. The average increase in wages and national income has accordingly been less than would otherwise have been possible.

The basis of this reasoning has often been attacked by protectionist advocates. No one knows how long the boom will continue, it is contended; when recessions occur again we shall also need those sectors which are weak at present, and meantime they must not be allowed to disintegrate under the pressure of foreign competition. We contest the validity of this argument, and refer the reader to Chapter II regarding the prospects for full employment.

Another form which the argument takes is that protection can make the country less sensitive to fluctuations in economic activity by giving it a more differentiated economic structure. 'Infant industry' duties are a reasonable device at the present day in the case of developing countries whose economies are dependent on one or a few staple commodities. But this has not been applicable to Sweden, at least since the turn of the century. The trouble with the Swedish economy at present, despite the recent liberalization of trade, is not that it has too much or too little variety, but that it has far too much of the *wrong* variety. Some of the older industries (not to mention agriculture, if more free trade were allowed there) suffering from over-capacity and dependent on tariff protection are severely hit by fluctuations in economic activity. If they could be contracted in size then recessions of the kind experienced in 1958, which must be expected to recur, would impose less of a strain.

(2) *The dumping and monopoly argument*

The demand for protection against dumping is a variation on the general employment argument for protection. Here the starting-point is the high fixed costs of modern industry. Capacity must be utilized as fully as possible in order to cover these, and this often leads to the dumping of exports at prices considerably below those of the home market, as long as they provide some surplus over and above, or at least cover, supplementary costs. 'Well-adjusted' tariff protection is then considered necessary in order to prevent the flooding of the domestic market. The importance of fixed costs is likely to go on increasing for a number of reasons, but if protective measures are adopted in this instance it is very easy to move towards general protection. In our view this is not the way to solve this problem. We must instead seek to have fewer and larger, more efficient and financially strong production units in the economy which can survive attacks of dumping and, when dumping is persistent, are able to change their type of production. Our proposals for tax and credit policy must be regarded from this point of view.

The argument about dumping prices is also put in a different way. If the foreign exporters are successful in decimating a Swedish industry by dumping they will, after the price war is over, recoup their losses through monopolistic exploitation of the Swedish market. Such fears are in our view totally unfounded. In 'traditional' branches of the economy exports usually stem from such different quarters as Eastern Europe and Asia, in addition to the industrial countries of the West, and there seems little or no likelihood of cartels being formed between such disparate interest groups. Through time these production conditions are likely to become more and more common in new, highly technical branches of industry as well, and this will naturally reduce the danger of international cartels in the long run. Instead of pursuing a protectionist policy within the country as a device against these, a conscious attempt ought on the contrary to be made to use a more liberal trade policy against monopolistic tendencies in Sweden, so that more competition can be forced on the economy.

(3) *The balance-of-payments argument*

Somewhat greater importance ought perhaps to be attached to the protectionist arguments which point at a country's balance of payments position. According to this way of thinking, high tariffs abroad restrict a country's own exports, and this forces it to limit its imports as well in order to avoid a deficit on the balance of trade. This argument exaggerates the rôle of tariffs in the total protection against imports which a country's economy enjoys; the foreign exchange position and various natural obstacles to imports are also important. In other words, a country with low tariffs can be in equilibrium, or even have a surplus, on her external account. In general, we maintain that in the short run an effective stabilization policy and appropriate exchange rates are more important for avoiding balance-of-payment deficits than higher tariffs.

It cannot be emphasized too strongly that in the long run this argument for protection is misleading. The damage has already been done when a foreign country has high tariffs or raises them at the expense of Swedish exports. Retaliation on the part of Sweden only accentuates the problem, for our cost level must then rise and our ability to export be further reduced.

A related argument to the one just discussed is that protection can help to improve the terms of trade. By limiting the demand for foreign goods and increasing domestic production this will help to reduce import prices and give better export prices abroad. This view originates in the USA, and it may possibly be of some general significance there, but hardly for a small country like Sweden. It is true that the argument may be valid for individual goods, but this need not of course affect the general level of tariffs.

Finally, the desire to use protection in order to achieve a more varied economy is traditionally justified on grounds of preparedness for war. This is a questionable argument. Military preparedness has meant attempting to maintain a peacetime level of production larger than is warranted by profitability in order to guarantee supplies in the event of blockade and war. This policy takes no account of the change in circumstances for Swedish production which has occurred as a result of the evacuation principles which the Riksdag approved in 1956. Now if large cities had to be evacuated—and this may be necessary whether or not a policy of neutrality is continued— a large proportion of our productive capacity could not be used, and it is therefore quite unrealistic to want to maintain a certain level of production for emergency purposes.

EUROPEAN INTEGRATION, THE UNDER-DEVELOPED COUNTRIES, AND INTERNATIONAL TRADE POLICY

The discussion has dealt so far mainly with the principles of international trade policy. We shall now enquire how far the above conclusions are affected by recent integration in Western Europe and by relations with the under-developed countries. These important matters have already been discussed in a general way in Chapter II, and here we shall take up some other aspects.

(1) *Integration and international trade constraints*

Our obligations under EFTA impose some limitations on Swedish international trade policy, and these constraints would certainly increase if more liberal trade were eventually to include the remainder of Western Europe as well. But whatever happens, we obviously still retain considerable freedom in our trade policy. Within EFTA, first of all, we retain it in relation to outside countries, with whom we can be as friendly as we like in the matter of free trade. Within a Western European customs union, on the other hand, we would be bound by its common tariff and trade policy in relation to countries outside the union. In that case Sweden could nevertheless work within the framework of the agreement for more liberal trade with non-member countries. Further, we would be able, as is the case at present within EFTA, to remove the obstacles to trade with other member states more rapidly than is required by the agreed phasing. No one can say, therefore, that we are, or will become, completely bound by the trade policy of other countries. How then ought we to use this freedom?

Our assessment of this question is based on our conviction that it would be unwise to exaggerate the pace and extent of the structural changes that can occur as a result of freer trade *within* Western Europe, even if it does tend to quicken the process. Six of the seven EFTA counties, Portugal being the exception, are rather similar in economic respects. They do not differ too much in their degree of industrialization and cost and price levels, and geographical distance and different languages operate as general impediments to trade. Among the Six as well economic differences are tending to be eliminated, and this ought also to have become true regarding comparisons between both European groups if any amalgamation of the two comes to pass. There is hardly any likelihood of a rapid economic revolution as a result of more liberal trade within West Europe, and this would probably also apply if North America were also to join later. Considerable differences in the degree of economic development have been able to persist within the USA, and they should be able to exist in any gigantic Western European trading bloc. Thus the structural transformation which appears probable as a result of EFTA or a possible Western European customs union need not appear too frightening to those who have a predilection for the *status quo*. Our conclusion is then that Sweden ought not simply to rest content with fulfilling any obligations that may arise, but that she should also use the freedom of action which we can count on retaining in order to pursue a policy favourable to free trade, which can in turn help to hasten the process of structural change.

Something ought also to be said about Sweden's position within two other international organizations, namely GATT (the General Agreement on Tariffs and Trade) and OECD (the Organization for Economic Co-operation and Development). It is true that the member countries of GATT fix their tariffs in relation to one another for a particular period of time, but they choose the level for these commitments independently, and Sweden is therefore not prevented by this agreement from conducting a policy of lowering tariffs. The justification given for the Government not doing this is that it is considered that Sweden ought—not least in the light of the negotiations for a Western European customs union—to seek primarily to reduce the differences in tariff levels in relation to the Six.

For our own part, we cannot agree with this. No one knows whether or when such a Customs Union can take place. If it does, it would very quickly mean that Sweden would have a lower level of tariffs, because the reduction of tariffs *within* the Union for more than two-thirds of our trade would weigh more heavily than the increases in our tariffs against non-member countries which we would then have to make. Thus there is no cause to depart from a low tariff line, for this would give Sweden a natural protection against imports in the form of a lower level of costs, instead of a tariff protection which would lead to a higher level of costs and restrict both imports and exports.

There is, finally, the question of OECD, the Organization for Economic Co-operation and Development, which has now replaced OEEC, and includes the countries of Western Europe as well as the USA and Canada. The precise forms of its work have not yet been determined, but we consider that within OECD Sweden ought to work, not simply by word but by deed, for a policy which favours free trade. In the immediate future, however, this organization's main concern will probably be help to the under-developed countries.

If, in the light of the above, one is still bold enough to predict increasingly rapid structural change during the present decade and thereafter, this is more because of developments outside the Western world. The Soviet Union and the other Communist States are undoubtedly growing more rapidly than the countries of EFTA and the USA. We can of course insulate ourselves from the direct competition of the Government trading of the Eastern countries with the help of import controls, and this is precisely what we are doing. But we do not avoid it in other markets, in practice in the under-developed countries. The rivalry between East and West in granting them credits will hasten their industrialization, and political competition will mean that it is not so easy in the future as it has been in the past for a country to insulate itself from trade with the under-developed countries and from the import of their cheap goods.

(2) *Trade groups and the under-developed countries*

Trade with the under-developed countries will therefore have to expand for a number of reasons. It will be advantageous not simply

101

on economic grounds, but also from the point of view of co-operation and international solidarity. Cultural exchanges often follow in the wake of trade.

If an expansion of trade is to be achieved, it is extremely important that the associations in Western Europe which are working for European economic co-operation should not be used in a protectionist way against the under-developed countries, as would happen if a high tariff wall were erected round these groups. The association in even stronger units of countries that are already strong economically can be regarded as a step forward for the whole world economy only if this combined strength is not used to discriminate against countries standing outside. Some years ago GATT expressed fears of such an outcome, and pointed out that if the European Economic Community were to develop into an instrument for distorting trade and increasing protection in relation to external agricultural products or other goods, this might be the signal for undesirable discriminatory arrangements emerging. In that case every country would lose, but in particular those which had no assured ways of selling their raw materials.

International trade integration in Western Europe carries with it the grave risk that the under-developed countries may be harmed. One example of the way in which organized co-operation between industrialized countries can operate is that imports by the OEEC countries from non-European countries in the period 1948–58 rose somewhat less than the total national product of the OEEC countries, while in the same period their exports to non-European countries increased twice as much and their internal trade more than three times as much as the national product.

The industrialized countries must appreciate these problems and seek to bring about improvements. A sympathetic attitude to free trade is not nearly systematic enough in the rich countries, and this must be fostered if it is to prove at all possible to solve the problems and bring about an improvement in the standard of living of the less-developed countries based on stable progress. Exports from these countries still consist predominantly of foodstuffs and natural industrial raw materials, for which world demand is rising less than world income, production, and total demand. This means that the relative prices of these goods are continually falling. From the point of view of foreign trade policy, therefore, it is essential for these countries to industrialize, both because of this slowing down in the rate of increase in demand and because of the pronounced cyclical fluctuations that occur in raw materials. The under-developed countries must obtain the necessary foreign exchange from the export of industrial goods as well so that they can continue expanding their industry.

(3) *The export of capital and export credits*

Although the under-developed countries must accept the primary responsibility themselves for meeting their capital requirements, they must be supplied with capital during a transitional phase if industrialization is to be promoted. This export of capital from the rich countries must in part—and in the foreseeable future it will be a very large part—take the form of long-term credits and direct investment. Sweden should be able to participate in this race to export capital as one aspect of the efforts by the industrial countries to alleviate the capital shortage in the less-developed countries, and also with a view to establishing trading relations with new and significant markets for Swedish products in the future.

The solution of these problems will require a large measure of co-operation between industry and the State. In some cases firms that are financially strong are capable of offering such credits, in others again the credit institutions can make the necessary credit facilities available. The export of capital to the less-developed countries on a sound financial footing should be one of the essential ways of supporting their industrialization, and the proposal to set up a special institute for the purpose of supplying medium or long-term export credits through borrowing on the capital market is one which we view with great satisfaction.[1]

Even if a private export finance institute were to be set up, however, some form of Government collaboration would probably be needed. The official Export Credits Board guarantees credits relating to exports to the under-developed countries, but this is conducted on a purely commercial basis, and in practice the stable markets are quite naturally favoured at the expense of markets where there are considerable risks, often of a political character. In our view official credit guarantees should instead be an instrument for supporting the under-developed countries, for example through reduced risk premiums and extended credit periods. It should be possible to fit help in this form into a comprehensive Swedish aid programme. Another idea is to extend the guarantees to include investment in the under-developed countries. This has been tried in practice in a number of countries, and could with advantage be examined in Sweden as well. Government investment guarantees would make it easier to establish Swedish subsidiaries in these countries, and in this case too aid could be combined with endeavours to create favourable conditions for expanding Swedish trade with these new markets.

(4) *More trade with the under-developed countries*

The industrialization of the under-developed countries will certainly

[1] This has now been done (1962).

be a lengthy process. New industries will in the first instance serve domestic markets, e.g. with textiles, and some of them will subsequently be able to produce a surplus for export. Relatively low labour costs will make their goods competitive with those of the industrial countries in many branches of light industry and to some extent in heavy industry as well. It is essential for these countries to benefit from the advantages of international specialization and division of labour. This will be of the greatest significance if their development is not to be hampered by chronic balance-of-payments difficulties. The industrial countries must then adopt a trade policy which is more favourably disposed to imports. It is desirable to ease the transition to these new conditions now, since the economies of the industrial countries will have to adjust in any event on the basis of EEC and EFTA. The main requirements in this context are greater adaptability on the part of the factors of production and more planning and Government influence in many fields.

An active labour market policy is required in order to ease the changeover that would result from a more liberal import policy, and this will require large resources both of finance and personnel. It is only reasonable that the industrial countries should have to solve some of the difficulties of adjustment caused by the dynamism of the world economy, for example by the use of labour market policy measures. It is necessary because the new industrial countries, with their weaker administrative apparatus, cannot be allowed to carry the whole burden of the problem of adjustment. Indeed it could be argued that resources used by an industrialized country to make its labour market more flexible are being used more effectively from the point of view of the world economy than the corresponding sums devoted to providing aid to an under-developed country which finds its exports to industrial countries blocked. If a more liberal trade policy is not pursued, aid will in the end culminate in something reminiscent of the inter-war German reparations problem. In the absence of large gold and foreign exchange reserves, the less industrialized countries must pay their debts through exports to the more mature industrial countries. If these are unwilling to open their markets to increased imports the only practical alternative is to write off the debts.

Since the industries of the less-developed countries are likely to be very weak in the immediate future, the requirement of a more liberal trade policy on the part of the established industrial countries should be combined, during the period of transition, with the concession to the young countries to protect their own weak industries during this phase. This of course is precisely what many of the industrial countries that are now highly developed did, not simply during the take-off stage of industrialism, but subsequently as well. Plans for the future expansion of the Swedish economy must take account of the under-developed countries' need for export markets, and we must ensure that the domestic economy grows rapidly enough for us to be able to allow a larger part of the expanding domestic market to be satisfied by these exports. Within OECD and other organizations, Sweden should be active in working for freer trade with the under-developed countries. If trade is not liberalized, aid to these countries will largely be in vain, and their economic expansion will be seriously retarded, a prospect which could do nothing but harm to the cause of democracy.

SUMMARY AND RECOMMENDATIONS

It is obvious from this discussion that it is difficult to find any tenable arguments in favour of Sweden pursuing a protectionist policy and maintaining tariffs. Although the increase in tariffs has been modest, and less than in many other countries, our conclusion is that this very tendency in international trade policy has nevertheless been an irrational one. Apart from the formation of the EFTA market by the seven member countries, the trend in tariffs has been quite the reverse of that regarded by LO as desirable. The current boom makes it perfectly proper to ask that the minimum tariffs introduced in the quite different economic circumstances of 1958 should be abolished. Tariffs should in addition have been reduced, for example in line with the views which LO expressed in 1956 on the report of the Committee on Tariffs. As we see it, the explanation of the failure to pursue a more explicitly liberal foreign trade policy must be sought in the authorities having shirked the problems of adjustment which such a policy would involve.

(1) *The trade union movement and international trade policy*

Like the working class movement as a whole, the trade unions have traditionally been sympathetic to free trade, although particular unions have frequently considered that they benefited from some protection in their own sector and low tariffs elsewhere! The explanation is not simply the desire to invoke some aid against unemployment that had already occurred, but also that a safeguard was sought against any possible future difficulties regarding wages and employment. As long as tariff decisions are made on a very long-term view, no guarantee can ever be given against employment and wage difficulties in the future, and it is understandable if trade unions then seek safeguards in the form of new or higher tariffs. Attempt of this kind were more natural before than under the post-war era of full employment, and the aim should now be to make them superfluous through appropriate institutional reforms.

We note with some pleasure that the Swedish trade union movement is more favourably disposed to free trade than is customary elsewhere, particularly if this Swedish outlook is compared with the protectionist ideas now current in the American trade union movement. Naturally, many factors have contributed to this difference in outlook, but one is particularly evident: the fundamental difference in the employment situation, general economic policy, and labour market policy. We regard this as clear proof that a policy which is favourable towards free trade can, at least in the long run, only be conducted against the background of full employment and full use of the possibilities that labour market policy affords. The trade union movement has a major task ahead of it in the application of a more liberal trade policy towards the under-developed countries. It is important here not to yield to protectionist fashions. Protectionist attitudes are often justified on the argument that conditions of work are unreasonable in the exporting countries. But arguments about 'dumping exports' and 'sweated labour competition' must not be accepted uncritically. Even if the object of protection is said to be the improvement of wages and working conditions in the under-developed countries, this cannot be done by obstructing their exports. It is also important for aid programmes to strengthen the trade union movement in these countries, e.g. through instruction in trade union organization.

(2) The co-ordination of international trade policy with economic policy

Departures from the free trade principle we have recommended *may* be justified under certain circumstances during a period of transition, if foreign competition really can be feared to lead to unemployment, or for the purpose of protecting an industry which has good prospects of becoming competitive on a longer view. But if such difficulties are encountered, it is by no means evident that they *ought* to be solved by raising tariffs or by similar measures. The choice often lies between a passive acceptance of more tariff protection and a more active economic policy in other respects. The latter alternative is undoubtedly preferable from a trade union point of view and raising tariffs only a last resort to prevent or counteract unemployment. In this connection we would like to emphasize strongly the need to ensure that changes within industry, whatever their cause, are made in a manner that is socially acceptable, and that effective labour market measures are adopted to protect the employees in the industry if necessary. The need for tariff increases will be less according as labour market, location and structural policies are more active.

Studies of the need for protection in particular branches of the economy have not paid sufficient attention to the connection that undoubtedly exists between the efficiency and competitive ability of individual enterprises and the particular industry's need for protection. The need can naturally vary from firm to firm. Just as the least efficient firms limit a sector's ability to pay higher wages and/or fix lower prices, so their need for protection is also greater. If a tariff is set at a level which allows the less efficient firms to survive, they may escape by the skin of their teeth, while the more efficient firms make excess profits. Long-term and unconditional tariff protection probably serves to weaken interest in structural rationalization, and thus it can readily help to maintain inefficient firms in an industry. If, however, demands for protection by producers are automatically linked to the demand that the structure of an industry should be rationalized, business firms will probably be more careful than they are at present about asking for more protection. This would no longer be given unless the firms undertook to accept certain obligations designed to reduce the need for protection.[1] To link the two aspects together in this way would probably be effective in restricting the demands for higher tariffs. In principle, tariffs are also comparable to subsidies, which should be officially controlled.

International trade policy has traditionally been treated in a separate compartment from the remainder of economic policy. From our point of view the connection with labour market policy is of particular interest, and it is worth recalling that when LO supported the proposal for a preparatory body on tariff questions put forward in a reservation to the report of the Committee on Tariffs, it was emphasized that the Labour Market Board and importers should be represented on it, as well as producers. LO argued that a body of this kind should collaborate with the labour market authorities and other institutions in putting forward proposals about methods of promoting structural rationalization through various tariff arrangements. However, the establishment of EFTA and the need to keep in step with the programme of tariff reductions by The Six have introduced new changes in the tariff field, at the same time as we have abandoned part of our freedom of action there, and the idea of a preparatory body on tariffs no longer seems necessary. Nevertheless, some forum is required for ensuring that the relationship between international trade policy and other parts of economic policy receives more attention in the future than it has been given in the past. Here, as with credit policy, the problem is to ensure that short-term official help does not degenerate into long-term subsidies. This is all the

[1] Cf. Chapter VI, on Credit Policy.

more important in the light of the new problems for international trade policy which will be posed by aid to the under-developed countries and an expansion of trade with them.

We doubt whether a special co-ordinating organization is needed in this case. The responsibility must rest largely with the Department of Industry and Employment which we have recommended. Organizational forms are not fundamental. What is important is that co-ordination should take place. In short, to vary a well-worn phrase, international trade policy is far too serious a matter to be entrusted to diplomats.

CHAPTER IX

COMPETITION, PRICES, AND
CONSUMER GUIDANCE

Official measures against restrictive practices, the general supervision of prices, and consumer guidance form three aspects of official attempts to create favourable conditions for economic progress. We regard these aspects of an expansionary economic policy as extremely important.

As a matter of fact, a policy favourable to competition and other measures to promote flexibility, such as labour market and capital market policy, are mutually conditioning. Even where the factors of production are very willing to adapt, the forces of progress are retarded if the pricing system does not function satisfactorily. On the other hand, it would be unreasonable to expect business men to abstain from restrictive practices and rigid methods of price fixing as long as the mobility of the factors of production is very limited. This relationship provides the starting-point for our examination of social measures dealing with restrictive practices, pricing, and consumer guidance. Our aim is to clarify the objectives of such social measures, and discuss whether they are adequate to meet the demands that may be made of them.

ACTION AGAINST HARMFUL RESTRICTIVE PRACTICES

The Swedish system for ensuring 'business freedom' from harmful restrictive practices differs from the corresponding legislation in a number of other countries by its flexible construction. In Sweden restrictive practices are, with very few exceptions, not unlawful in themselves, but it must first be shown in each individual case that the particular limitation on competition is harmful in its effects. Once this has been established, it is the function of the Freedom of Commerce Board to endeavour to have it removed. If this cannot be achieved through negotiation, the only remaining course is to report the position to the Government.

No attempt is made in the Act to define the concept of 'restrictive practice'. The legislators have not aimed at trying to bring about free competition in the conventional sense of the term, but primarily at ensuring a high degree of '*effective*' *competition*, in the sense that it is possible for a purchaser to choose among different goods and different sources of supply, and thereby to influence quality, price, and service. This of course requires the existence of several sellers who do compete seriously on price, quality, and service, all things which can be considered to satisfy a widely varying demand.

It follows from the above that the intention is not to counter all restrictions on competition, but only those which harm consumers. A restrictive practice is deemed harmful if it from the public point of view unduly affects pricing, obstructs the operation of the economic system, and/or impedes or prevents the pursuit of economic activity by another party.

It is the task of the Commissioner for Freedom of Commerce and the Freedom of Commerce Board to show that one or all of these criteria are satisfied before a particular procedure is to be considered harmful within the meaning of the Act. In two cases, however, collective tendering and resale price maintenance, the burden of proof has been reversed, and a harmful effect has been presumed. Thus these procedures are generally prohibited, and infringement of the provisions can lead to prosecution in the public courts, although the Freedom of Commerce Board can grant dispensations from these prohibitions.

The policy is administered by three independent instances, an investigating body (the State Price and Cartel Office), a body which corresponds most closely to the public prosecutor (the Commissioner for Freedom of Commerce), and a judicial instance (the Freedom of Commerce Board).

It is the duty of the Board 'to follow developments in, and promote general knowledge about, prices and competitive conditions in business'. It is an investigating body, and not an executive agency for the control of prices and competition. For that part of the work of investigation relating to restrictive practices in business, the Board functions in part as a service agency for the Commissioner. In addition, one of its tasks is to compile the public register of cartels. In this connection it also undertakes detailed investigations into restrictive trade agreements which may be presumed to have socially harmful consequences.

The procedure before the Business Freedom Council is set in motion in the first instance by the Commissioner. Only if he has decided in a particular case not to call for examination are entrepreneurs immediately affected by the restrictive practice, or associations of consumers or wage earners, entitled to ask for such a hearing.

It is of course important, if the legislation is to have the desired effect, for the Commissioner to obtain knowledge about the existence of restrictive practices which can be assumed to give rise to abuses. The Commissioner has four main sources of information at his disposal, (a) investigations conducted by the Price and Cartel Board, (b) information about restrictive agreements contained in the register of cartels, (c) applications from entrepreneurs or consumers who consider they are being harmed by certain restrictive practices, and (d) information in the daily press and journals which arouses suspicions that a restrictive practice is harmful in a particular case.

If a limited enquiry is all that is necessary in order to enable the Commissioner to arrive at a view about a particular question, this is generally conducted by his own staff. Otherwise, the Commissioner can ask the State Price and Cartel Office to make a special enquiry. If examination by the Freedom of Commerce Board has been called for, a procedure then comes into operation which is largely reminiscent of that of the public courts. If the Board finds that a restrictive practice is harmful, it decides to try to have the harmful effect removed through discussion and negotiation. The Board cannot issue binding instructions, but simply recommend the parties to take the action it finds appropriate.

(1) *Experience of this legislation*

It is of course difficult to say precisely how much competition and rigidity exist in business, and what changes have occurred since the legislation on restrictive practices was introduced. Although there have been signs of more lively and price-conscious competition in recent years, it is practically impossible to say how much of this is a result of the action by the authorities in supervising prices and competition, and how much is attributable to other circumstances. The legislation has, however, undoubtedly had some effect.

Of the 1,800 agreements registered so far about half have been abandoned, probably because the agreements have been made public through the process of registration. The prohibition of resale price maintenance and collective tendering has also been very important. The prohibition of resale price maintenance has made possible new forms of distribution which use the price as the chief method of competition, and in this way even well established brands could be, and have been, the subject of severe price competition in retail trade. In certain trades, however, maintained prices have been replaced by recommended prices. The retailers can, it is true, charge less than these prices, but the tendency to follow the recommended prices has proved so strong in many cases that one can in fact speak of a continuation of the system of resale price maintenance. Here the authorities have been less successful in keeping a watching brief on prices.

The Swedish legislation on restrictive practices may, with the exception of the special cases mentioned above, appear weak and ineffective. The Freedom of Commerce Board can only resort to negotiation in its endeavours to remove the harmful effects of a particular

111

restrictive practice. As suggested, if a satisfactory result cannot be achieved in this way, the only course is to report the matter to the Government, but in practice this has not yet occurred. In twenty-two of the forty-five cases of restrictive practices which came before the Board in some form in the period 1954 to July 1961, it was possible to reach agreement between the parties before the stage of negotiation was reached. On the other hand, this tendency on the part of business firms to reach agreement before the Freedom of Commerce Board has arrived at a final view about the issue means there are very few test cases where a decision can serve as a precedent. The limited resources at the disposal of the investigating and 'prosecuting' bodies have also kept the number of cases examined to a minimum. As a rule, the Commissioner and the Council have intervened as a result of notification from aggrieved business men, not on the initiative of the Board or the Commissioner. The possibility of intervening against unreasonable price fixing by prescribing maximum prices has not been used so far.

(2) *Should the burden of proof be reversed?*

The theory underlying legislation on restrictive practices in business is that free competition between business enterprises leads as a rule to rationalization and improvements in efficiency which can benefit the consumer in the form of lower prices and better quality. At the same time, the condition that only restrictive practices which have manifestly harmful effects should be the subject of official intervention indicates that the legislator is not condemning out of hand every form of deviation from the narrow path of free competition. Since the Act contains no definition of the concept 'restrictive practice', an idea of its coverage can only be obtained from a study of the preliminaries. The most important examples are cartels, monopolies, oligopolies, branded goods, vertical fixed prices, discriminating sales and price discrimination. As the above list shows, practically every case of restrictive practice can be reported and lead to action on the part of the authorities.

We share the 'pragmatic' view underlying Swedish legislation in this area, namely that a clear definition of what is to be regarded as a harmful restrictive practice is not possible, and that an obvious restrictive practice, e.g. in the form of a cartel agreement, is not in itself evil; whether a particular measure has harmful effects is a matter that must be judged on the merits of each particular case. It is, however, a weakness that the burden of proof rests with the authorities; the original proposal of a 'reversed burden of proof' meant that the individual firm or the firms that were parties to an agreement would instead have to show that the restrictive practice was not harmful to the public interest. Placing the burden of proof here would, in our view, increase the efficiency of the Government's measures to promote competition. One of the consequences of giving the Act more teeth would undoubtedly be that compulsory measures would have to be used to a greater extent than has been the case so far.

However, the possibilities of using legislative compulsion to ensure a high degree of competition or inflict a decisive defeat on fixed pricing are probably very limited. What can be done officially is to use a variety of means to remove or mitigate the obvious effects of limitations on competition, and in this way create more favourable conditions for the willingness to compete to find expression. On the other hand, legislation, however well conceived, can never influence the willingness to compete as such. Complementary measures of another kind are necessary for this purpose, namely effective supervision of prices, and active consumer guidance. Indeed, restrictive practices legislation can never be looked at in isolation from these two other groups of measures. Restrictive practices legislation, the supervision of prices, and consumer guidance together form a whole, and their common task is to facilitate and make possible flexible pricing and the adjustment of the economy to the ever changing conditions of the market.

ACTION AGAINST PRICE RIGIDITIES

The need for Government price controls during periods of crisis when there is a marked shortage of goods and speculative tendencies are rife has never been seriously contested, but the necessity for price control in normal circumstances, when imports are free and there is a plentiful supply of goods, has been the subject of much debate. The existing arrangements, which are based mainly on the proposals put forward in 1955 by a Committee of Enquiry into price controls,[1] provide that price controls can be resorted to in times of war and blockade, and in clearly inflationary situations. In normal times, however, it is considered that competition can be relied upon as the regulator of prices. At the time price control proper was swept away, the Minister of Trade indicated there was a *quid pro quo*, in the form of increased powers to intervene against restrictive practices in the economy, the supervision of prices, and greater consumer guidance.

The unions long resisted the abolition of price controls, and LO has argued on a number of occasions since the war that continuous surveillance of prices in association with direct price controls cannot

[1] S.O.U. 1955:45, *Konkurrens och priser* (Competition and Prices).

be avoided even in periods when the economy is comparatively stable. LO argued that it was necessary in a full employment economy for the Government to have powers to intervene in price fixing, although price control can and ought simply to be complementary to fiscal and monetary policy and measures against restrictive practices. LO only accepted the proposal for a changeover from price controls to the supervision of prices in the light of the tremendously improved prospects for combining the supervision of prices and control of restrictive practices which the proposal aimed at providing.

Since the new legislation came into force and the State Price and Cartel Office began its activities there have been a number of occasions on which the trade unions have requested more official action to restrain the tendency for prices to rise. LO expressed this opinion most clearly in a submission to the Government in 1960 demanding more efficient surveillance of prices. LO did not wish to see a return to war time and emergency price controls, and was willing to believe that in the business sector the readiness to compete was as a rule sufficiently strong to make this unnecessary. What LO wanted was not new powers, but above all an increase in the personnel available for the task of supervising prices.

A committee was appointed, and in 1961 the Riksdag agreed to a sizeable increase in the personnel available for this purpose. Together with the increase in staff which the State Price and Cartel Office obtained in connection with the introduction of the turnover tax, this has meant that enough staff are probably available now to enable the work of investigation and publicity to be conducted on a reasonable scale.

LO had also argued that the authorities seemed to have far too narrow powers of intervention in cases of palpably unreasonable price fixing, and it has now been made clear that the authorities also have power under the existing arrangements to intervene against unreasonable price fixing and to decree maximum prices. This should remove one of the obscurities in the interpretation of the Restrictive Practices Act.

There will always be practical difficulties in the way of proving unreasonable price fixing. But when it can be proved, the ultimate explanation is as a rule probably to be found in some form of imperfect competition, which then makes it possible to decree maximum prices. A broad interpretation of the legal provision about measures against unreasonable pricing could be that a price may be unreasonable not merely if it is unreasonably high in relation to costs but also if the *costs* are unreasonably high, i.e. if the structure of the enterprise or the branch is irrational. We consider it is very valuable for the statute to be given this wide interpretation and to be used in practice in a way which makes it an instrument of pricing based on free competition and on a rational structure of the economy.

Another question of principle is that of the rules regarding secrecy. The Minister of Trade has emphasized that it may be quite defensible, in the more sensational or important cases, to publish current information about prices and other conditions for a particular enterprise, of which the name is made public. This should be used with caution, though caution should not be carried to excessive lengths. This statement by the Minister should make it possible in our view for the State Price and Cartel Office to abandon the reluctance it has shown on this point. As far as is known, there has not been a single case, however scandalous or important it may have been, where public attention has been drawn to the price fixing of an individual firm. This should be changed, since specific intimations of this kind constitute a necessary part of effective consumer information.

Our position with regard to social measures on pricing can be summarized in the following way. Price control in the strict sense ought not normally to be used in an economy where imports are free and there is an ample supply of goods. It cannot, however, be assumed that, in an economy in which the resources of production are as a rule fully utilized and purchasing power is high and continually rising, pricing will always follow the laws of the market. As a matter of fact, there is considerable scope for 'cost plus' pricing. The price flexibility which forms part of the picture of a freely competitive economy only finds a small echo in the real world. It is not sufficient for the Government to protect the consumer and business enterprise against monopolistic phenomena. Permanent and active surveillance of prices is necessary in addition and, in the last resort, it ought to be possible to use price controls as the ultimate corrective.

This may be even more applicable in future. True, the general opinion is that a growing stream of foreign goods will tend to intensify competition and reduce prices; but this overlooks the point that the variety of goods may be large, and difficult for the consumer to assess. Official policy ought therefore to pay close attention to their pricing. Other points which argue in favour of the maintenance of, and even the extension of, price supervision are the greater flexibility with regard to tariffs, indirect taxation and agricultural price fixing.

If this supervision of prices is to be effective, it ought not simply to operate through investigations into the prices, margins, and costs of various firms and branches. The results should also be made available to the public through widespread publicity. Consumer information is one of the most important, although in practice it is the weakest, links in the chain of social measures to promote competition.

INCREASING CONSUMER INFORMATION

The provision of consumer information is very widely scattered among a number of institutions. These overlap to some extent, and there is no strict division between institutions concerned with research and those which disseminate the results of research. Some regard consumer information as their main job, while for others it is a more marginal part of their activity. Some are independent of any commercial interest, while others exist primarily to promote a particular group of goods or the product of a particular manufacturer.

In addition to the State Price and Cartel Office, the independent bodies include the National Consumers' Council, which is a general advisory and research-sponsoring body in this field. The National Institute for Consumer Information carries on research and information, and the VDN—Institute for Informative Labelling—which consists of representatives of business, the interest organizations and consumers, devises declarations for the standards of goods. There are also private organizations which devote themselves to consumer information, e.g. the women's sections of the political parties, the Housewives' Association, the Women's Guild of the Co-operative Union, and the Swedish Handicraft Association. The total effort of the official institutions is, however, very limited and by no means matches up to the objective which was indicated in the report of the price control committee, namely that the achievement of more effective competition necessitated doing everything possible to increase the opportunities for consumers to assess the market through greater knowledge of goods and prices. Consumer information with this double aim was said to be a prerequisite of the abolition of price controls.

It is only since the Riksdag decided in 1961 to increase the staff of the information section of the State Price and Cartel Office that the demand for more information can be said to have been satisfied to some modest extent as regards prices. Information of other kinds about goods is available only very sparsely through the official institutions just mentioned, and there is practically no co-ordination of information about prices and quality.

We have no hesitation in stating that the official contribution in the sphere of consumer information is quite inadequate. About 2 per cent of our national income, or about 1,000 m. crowns a year, is used for advertising which is in part informative but almost overwhelmingly persuasive and tendentious. The growing flood of goods means that consumers increasingly require objective information and guidance. It is not simply a question of products increasing in number, for with a rising standard of welfare the more expensive and complicated durable consumer goods occupy an increasingly important place in our total consumption. In relation to this growing need for information the contribution of the public authorities remains insignificant, amounting to less than one per cent of what private enterprise devotes to advertising. It is no exaggeration when the committee on the supervision of prices observes in its report that practically nothing has been done so far in the field of consumer information. Talk about the consumer as the central figure in our economy is completely misleading, and simply wishful thinking. The consumer's choice is still based only to a very slight extent on knowledge and rational consideration, and it can be strongly influenced by the sellers' arguments, which are framed not so much by the endeavour to provide objective information about goods as by the compulsion to assert themselves in competition.

Consumer information has a two-fold aim: it must cultivate a more active and independent attitude on the part of the consumer, and it must give concrete information which is of value to the consumer confronted with various purchasing situations. We recommend greatly enlarged official contributions in both these areas. This will probably have to be preceded by scientific research into the methodology of fostering better consumer education. This is a comparatively new area, with no research traditions and no powerful and well-financed interests providing stimulus and support. Consumer research ought therefore to be given much more Government support than it has received so far, and research of this kind ought to have a more definite place in our universities. The situation is somewhat more favourable for the scientific testing of different products, although the shortage of research staff, funds and material equipment does limit very considerably the range of products that can be subjected to continuous testing. It is desirable to extend the range of the products covered, to develop a system of awarding points for as many products as possible according to their different qualities, and to publicize the results of these tests, with an indication of the product's name and price.

More information about prices through the Price and Cartel Board ought now to be possible as a result of the increase in staff. But in this area as well one can distinguish between general information activity designed to inform the consumer and information which can be of direct use to consumers in specific situations. The latter has so far been completely neglected. The Price and Cartel Board should, for example, carry out regional and local studies of the spread of prices for particular goods. Activity of this kind would be more effective if collaboration with the trade unions could be developed.

Hitherto in Sweden, in contrast to a large number of other countries, consumer research and consumer information have been considered matters primarily for the authorities, and there has not been any need for exclusive consumer organizations so far. The probable reasons for this are that in Sweden we have at least the beginnings of Government activity in this area, a strong consumer co-operative movement, willingness on the part of industry to collaborate on consumer questions, and an attitude to advertising which is more favourably disposed to the consumer than in some other countries. But if the Government continues to show insufficient interest in consumer information it is likely that the idea of forming pure consumer organizations, devoted to conducting research, testing goods, and expressing opinions, will gain in strength. While this would necessarily lead to some dissipation of forces, and is not one that we would recommend, we cannot dismiss the idea as unreasonable. It is a second-best alternative to a co-ordinated effort along the lines followed hitherto, but on a considerably enhanced scale. But it provides a better alternative than the inadequate official effort that is being made in this sphere at the present time.

CHAPTER X

LABOUR MARKET AND LOCATION POLICY

THE CURRENT LABOUR MARKET POLICY

The practical aspects of labour market policy are the responsibility of a special Government department, the Labour Market Administration, which is headed by the National Labour Market Board.[1] The Board takes charge of the central administration, the County Labour Boards, Employment Exchanges, and the workplaces and stores of the Administration. It has a staff of about 3,000.

During the recession which became quite pronounced in the course of 1958 labour market policy was given increasing prominence in economic policy, and a big increase was made in the grant at the disposal of the Labour Market Board for counteracting the decline in employment. Emphasis was still placed on the old, traditional labour market policy measures, such as emergency works and cash payments to the unemployed, but an opportunity was also given for experimenting with new methods of providing employment for those seeking work. People began more and more to speak about the 'new' labour market policy. It is no exaggeration to say that this new element has been inspired largely by statements and representations from LO. Thus as early as 1951 the LO enquiry entitled *Trade Unions and Full Employment*[2] was outlining the framework for modern labour market policy.

Current policy makes use of a larger number of weapons and operates over a wider range of the economy than it did previously. The distinguishing characteristic of the 'new' policy is 'active' intervention, by methods which are as selective as possible, to provide help in the sectors where it is needed and in the manner best suited to each particular case. There is much less emphasis on the passive announcement of new job opportunities and more on active measures to influence both labour and enterprises in a particular direction.

This activity can be divided roughly into the following main groups:

[1] The Board consists of a Director General (chairman), a Deputy, a Chief Engineer, and seven members appointed by the Government from among trade unions and employers' organizations.

[2] This report was submitted to the LO congress of 1951 under the title *Fackföreningsrörelsen och den fulla sysselsättningen.* An abbreviated English translation with the above title was published in 1953.

(1) Forecasting, and planning measures against unemployment, e.g. the collection and working up of statistics and planning suitable work projects.

(2) Unemployment insurance and unemployment relief.

(3) Measures to create employment, e.g. emergency works, the placing of orders with firms experiencing employment difficulties to enable them to maintain production during a difficult period, and the provision of work for handicapped workers.

(4) Measures to stimulate geographical mobility, through the labour exchanges, including the granting of removal and family allowances, starting allowances, and various financial inducements to increased geographical mobility; and occupational mobility, through vocational training, further training and re-training.

The measures designed to create employment, particularly emergency works and unemployment relief, are still by far the main cost items. Despite the increased emphasis in recent years on action to stimulate mobility, this still accounts for only a very small part of the total cost of labour market policy.

A MORE FLEXIBLE LABOUR MARKET

(1) More efficient job placement

One of the basic assumptions of our programme is that full employment can be maintained. A shortage rather than a surplus of labour will therefore tend to be the common state of affairs, and this will accentuate the need for efficiency in the use of the labour available. We also expect significant changes in the geographical distribution of industry and in the nature of production and work processes. This will make new demands on employees and on their skills and training, but it will also bring about a new situation regarding employment possibilities in different areas and regions of the country. Efficiency will therefore require a more flexible labour market, and it is the responsibility of labour market policy to make the adjustments that became necessary both attractive and rewarding for the employees through positive measures to stimulate movement.

The basic and essential activity in this connection is an *active job placement service*. The movement of labour in a particular direction and the ironing-out of discrepancies between surplus and deficit areas of the labour market presuppose accurate and detailed information about the real conditions. Where is labour needed, of what kind, what are the earnings prospects, is housing available, what are the conditions of work, what sort of community is it? An *active job information service* of this kind is probably sufficient to satisfy the majority of the cases where the need for adjustment arises.

120

In principle this is not new. The labour exchanges are already well tried and developed in Sweden, but still more can and ought to be done in this field, and still more resources and interest must be devoted to them in the future. Above all, this work should be directed more towards the structural shifts in the economy. People seeking work who already have jobs, but who wish for one reason or another to change their jobs, must be given help. The general objective must be to treat the various applications for jobs on an individual basis. Each individual must be given help so that he himself can make a realistic analysis of his position and then arrive at a rational decision about his choice of future workplace or occupation.

In many places the labour market authorities are represented by part-time officials and, understandably enough, it is less easy for them to provide the help applicants need, and still less possible for them to take the initiative in making contacts themselves. In such regions, which are usually sparsely populated areas or small towns, there are strong obstacles to mobility and a great need for active labour market policy measures. In some cases the labour market authorities have tried to solve this problem by temporarily strengthening the labour exchange organization in particular districts where unemployment is rife. Thus staff from the industrial areas of central and southern Sweden have on occasion been sent to various parts of Upper Norrland. So far this approach has yielded very favourable results and it seems to be a method which should continue to be used in future. If the labour exchange service is to become an active stimulus to movement and provide individual service, the numbers and quality of staff must, however, be markedly increased.

(2) *Economic stimuli to increased mobility*

The informative announcement of vacancies and improved labour exchange facilities cannot, however, solve all the problems of adjustment. In areas where economic activity is undeveloped there will still be too many people in relation to the employment opportunities which can be offered there, while at the same time there may be a troublesome shortage of labour in other parts of the country or other sectors. This geographical immobility of labour may have several explanations. In some cases the reasons which tie a person to a particular place or area are overwhelmingly economic in character, such as the ownership of a house which cannot be sold without loss, high removal costs, difficulties of obtaining a house in the proposed job area, and so on. But the strongest obstacles to increased mobility are frequently social and psychological in character, e.g. the unwillingness to change acquired habits and to lose a long-standing circle of acquaintances. In many cases too a person may perhaps be unable to move to another place because of age, ill-health, or a lack of training.

It has already been argued that labour market policy must use positive measures so that the necessary mobility appears both attractive and rewarding. This is easiest when the obstacles to mobility are basically economic in character. It is always possible for the community, if it is willing, to compensate the individual for the financial sacrifice involved in a geographical job transfer. To this end, a large number of different routes have been explored in recent years, such as travelling money, family allowances, and starting allowances. However, these financial stimuli must be used selectively, for it would be unreasonable to give every one who changed his job or place of activity special social compensation. At present financial allowances are paid on the merits of each individual case, and it seems appropriate to continue on this basis.

This type of activity, which is still experimental in character, must nevertheless be expanded considerably if the anticipated need for greater mobility on the part of the labour force is to be satisfied in ways which are socially acceptable. It is still frequently the case that a person who loses his job as a result of the structural changes that are continually taking place could obtain new employment in another place where there is a shortage of labour, but he does not move because he could not obtain full financial compensation for the move. This forces the authorities to resort to much more expensive employment policy measures, such as unemployment assistance or emergency works, which only solve the unemployment problem temporarily, in contrast to what would happen if workers moved to an expanding region. Even if it is necessary in some cases to pay considerably larger sums in order to get this desired movement under way, it nevertheless appears a very good investment for the community as a whole.

It is not simply the amount of financial assistance, but also the restrictive regulations surrounding its disbursement, which reduces its effectiveness as a stimulus to movement. As a rule, a person must be unemployed in order to be eligible for assistance. This link with the concept of unemployment is a relic of the time when labour market policy was in essence an unemployment policy, and it may have unfortunate effects from the structural point of view. It may frequently be the case that the labour released is for a variety of reasons extremely difficult to move, while it is easier to transfer workers who have not lost their jobs in a particular place. If the labour that is released can obtain employment in this way in its own area, it is clearly sensible to allow those who are not unemployed but are willing to move to obtain the financial allowance instead. So far these contributions have only been paid in a small number of the interlocality moves. Apart from the restraining effect of the rules themselves and the examination procedure which is necessary for payment to be made, the explanation probably lies in the fact that the responsible authorities—the County Labour Boards and in some cases the managers of the labour exchanges—have not yet fully realized the need for an active stimulus to greater mobility. It is not enough for the sources of finance to exist. They must also be known to those for whom movement is or ought to be a live issue. Better information from the side of the labour market authorities about the financial grants, advice, and other services available is therefore necessary.

(3) *Housing and the mobility of labour*

The housing question has been and still is a tremendous obstacle in the way of a labour market policy designed to stimulate mobility. It is a problem that concerns both the place from which labour moves and the place to which it moves. In the place from which labour is moving the problem arises through very many workers owning their own homes. If these are situated in an area with a bad employment position it is frequently difficult to find purchasers who are willing to pay what the house is worth to the person living there. The probability of a loss on sale is a strong deterrent to moving, and it delays and obstructs adjustments to the employment situation which would otherwise be possible. It is important that this obstacle should be removed. Action by the authorities is needed here in order to facilitate the sale of such property. In addition to help in the form of providing contacts with interested purchasers, consideration should be given to the direct purchase of the house, or to the authorities standing guarantee for the difference between the value of the property to the owner and the amount that can be obtained for it when it is sold. The Labour Market Board has asked the Government for permission to experiment in this field, but so far this has not been granted. A systematic and active labour market policy does, however, require that the authorities obtain the resources and powers to intervene in this respect as well.

Complementary to this activity, there must in future be greater emphasis on economic policy aspects in the distribution of loans for owner-occupier housing. Such housing loans ought not to be granted in places where a great deal of troublesome structural unemployment exists or can be expected to arise in the foreseeable future.

The difficulty of obtaining housing, especially for families, is the main obstacle to mobility in those regions which are expanding and seeking labour. The labour market authorities have tried in some cases to solve this problem by having temporary housing built for letting. Although this has, it is true, made possible an increased flow of labour to certain areas of shortage and at the same time has alleviated employment difficulties in other areas, the method does have disadvantages, and is not really a long-term solution.

What is needed instead is a big increase in the new housing quotas in expanding areas. Here too the authorities have experimented to some extent in recent years. During the autumn of 1960 a number of places in which there was a shortage of both houses and labour and where housing projects had been prepared did obtain permission from the Housing Board to begin the building of houses which could not be included in the loan budget originally drawn up for the authorities in that financial year, on condition that these houses were made available for unemployed workers who moved in from other places. This seems to be a solution which should be used more extensively in future.

Here, however, as in the case of the purely financial stimuli to mobility, strict priority in the allocation of housing to the unemployed may hamper flexible adjustment. It may well happen that the unemployed workers from a declining area are not the type required in an expanding area. If firms were able to utilize the extra housing quota in recruiting labour of another kind and from a different quarter, the unemployed from the first area might easily obtain new employment despite, or perhaps because of, this. In the allocation of housing the authorities ought therefore to have a fairly free hand in promoting 'triangular exchanges'.

(4) *Adapting labour to new surroundings*

Although it is more difficult, and in some cases perhaps impossible, to remove the social and psychological obstacles to mobility, the labour market authorities must also endeavour to provide compensation for the psychological 'cost', and make mobility not simply acceptable but also attractive. The process of adjustment is not completed when workers have been induced to move from their original surroundings to jobs elsewhere. More attention must be paid to resettlement in the new job and locality. Job information and induction, information about the new community, the type of housing and its location, contacts with other people, associations and clubs of various kinds, are all important aspects. The resources at the disposal of the authorities have not so far been sufficient to give this side of the process the necessary emphasis, and they must be increased. One possibility is to have special consultants, whose job it would be to help workers to adjust to the new environment. If a group of people move simultaneously from one area to another it may be particularly appropriate to make a close study of the adjustment process in order to gain experience of the effect various stimuli have had, and discover ways of correcting and refining the methods used.

Management must carry the main responsibility for job induction, but the trade unions could also make a valuable and positive contribution. They already do so in many cases. Closer and more extensive collaboration between the labour market authorities, management, and trade unions is, however, desirable in the reception and adjustment of new labour both to the job and the whole social environment. It must be remembered that environment, background of experience, and habits can vary so tremendously, even among Swedish workers, that special measures are needed to ensure a successful outcome.

(5) *Occupational mobility*

The main emphasis so far as been on the need to increase geographical mobility of labour, but there will be a need in the future for greater occupational mobility as well. The essential foundation for this is a better general school education, which allows greater choice in the selection of occupation and facilitates further special training or a later transfer to another type of employment if the first choice of occupation has proved an unhappy one. The current revision of the elementary school system will clearly bring an improvement in this respect.

A broadly based general educational system will not, however, in itself be a sufficient foundation for the specialized labour market of the future. Business firms demand greater craft skills on the part of their labour but, despite the considerable educational expansion in this area in recent years, the resources here are still quite inadequate. The community must be prepared to invest much more in this work in the future.

Persons already in employment who have not had the advantage of this improved basic education may also wish to change their jobs or be faced with the need to do so. This necessitates retraining or, if the person in question has had no previous occupational training, basic training. The current activity of the labour market authorities in this field, which takes the form of short courses and financial grants to compensate those who are undergoing training for the loss of income during the course, thus fulfils a useful function and will become increasingly important. Despite the special attention which this part of labour market policy has enjoyed in recent years, however, a further expansion of capacity and resources in this area appears particularly desirable, both with regard to the amount of the training grants and the rules for their payment, and the number of places and the types of training offered. Here too it may be quite rational to extend the system by allowing non-wage earners, and persons who are not unemployed but who nevertheless wish to learn a new trade, to obtain financial grants during their period of training. Women who wish to return to the labour market after some years of work at home, but whose previous skills have been outmoded or who have had no occupational training at all, form a particularly important group in this connection.

(6) *Handicapped workers*

It is conceivable that more extensive structural changes in the economy and a policy to stimulate adaptability may lead, at least temporarily, to an increase in that group of workers who are not easily placed in jobs. The labour market authorities must show more interest in this question, both on humanitarian and economic grounds. Elderly and female workers raise particular problems here, since the obstacles to mobility are largely psychological in character, such as pre-conceived notions on the part of employers about the ability of elderly and female workers to undertake new tasks, and also on the part of the workers themselves regarding their capacity for learning new proficiencies or adjusting to a new environment. The main way to overcome these obstacles must be through an intensive information campaign, to which the trade unions can also make an important contribution.

Female workers in particular may have special requirements with regard to hours of work and the nature of the workplace, and firms must be induced to offer more part-time work. There must be more nurseries for children with working mothers. The organizational and economic problems here could be solved by collaboration between business firms, the Labour Market Administration, and the local authorities.

If structural change continues to lead to a concentration of economic activity and population in more densely populated areas, the prospects of providing suitable jobs for elderly and female workers ought, however, to be simplified through the richly varied labour market which may then arise. A continuation of full employment will also ease the employment problems of these groups.

CURRENT LOCATION POLICY

There is a very close connection between labour market and location policy. They may be alternatives; men are taken to jobs, or firms are taken to places where men are unemployed. In other cases they may be complementary; both men and firms are attracted to areas with the best prospects of expansion. When the Riksdag decided some years ago to experiment with industrial location it was therefore quite appropriate that the responsibility for this should be assigned to the Labour Market Board.

The work of the authorities regarding the location of individual industrial enterprises is mainly informative, advisory, and investigatory in character. In addition, the location bureau, which is part of the Labour Market Board, collaborates with the County Labour Boards and other bodies in investigating the structure and development of economic activity and population in various parts of the country. Thus in the period 1946–58 the Labour Market Board and its agencies assisted in the location of about 230 undertakings[1] with 25,000 employees.

The drift from the countryside and the rapid growth of the large towns are still the main problems for Government location policy. In some quarters it is often argued that this concentration of economic activity in large population centres is open to objection, while others have pointed out that the advantages claimed for the dispersion of economic activity are often unrealistic and exaggerated.

A number of other problems relating to this question require attention. Many regions need a more varied economic structure if they are to be less sensitive to economic fluctuations, if women as well as men are to obtain employment, and if young people are to have a wider choice of occupations. Further, the closing down of industrial firms can create difficult local problems which necessitate some action from the side of location policy. From the defence point of view as well, location is important.

The aims of the Government's current location policy were set out in legislation of 1952. 'Location policy ought to be co-ordinated with the efforts to utilize to the full the available resources of manpower and to support the expansion of economic activity in those places where total costs are least.' Advice and information, aimed at 'clarifying for business men the social and economic conditions which the Government considers should be taken into account in determining location', were regarded as the appropriate weapons of Government policy for influencing the location of private firms. Individual grants by the State and local authority subsidies as means of influencing location were not considered desirable, although a system of permits to prevent unsuitable location was not considered necessary.

[1] Of these, about sixty moved from the Greater Stockholm area, and about thirty from Gothenburg.

Advisory activity in this field is also carried on by a private institution, the Production Council for Industry, which is a joint body sponsored by the Swedish Employers' Confederation and the Federation of Swedish Industries, and one of its duties is to provide a service to business firms on industrial location questions.

Besides the advisory activity of the labour market authorities, the Government can influence the location of economic activity in other ways, both directly and indirectly. Some account is taken of location aspects in the allocation of Government loans to associations of business firms. Town planning, the siting of houses, and the course of water and drainage facilities are of crucial importance in locating business enterprises within a particular region, but they are also very important for the distribution of economic activity between different areas of the country. Other factors over which there is a great degree of official control and to which regard is paid in decisions about the establishment of or re-location of a firm are the network of public communications, the intensity of traffic, the power supply and other public enterprises, schools, and local health and hospital facilities. Finally, the wage and tax 'zones' into which the country is divided can be significant factors in a businessman's choice of location.[1]

A MORE EFFICIENT LOCATION POLICY

The problems of location policy must be assessed from a national point of view. Many places and areas can show commendable reasons for augmenting industrial activity. There may be places with troublesome unemployment, an unbalanced and cyclical economic structure, or firms which have stagnated. However, not every locality in the country can have its desire to expand satisfied, and in the long run dispersion of business enterprise would seriously hamper our efforts to bring about a rapid rise in the material standard of living.

Thus location policy should aim at allocating enterprises to those places where they can be economically viable. This is not simply a question of obtaining as large a surplus as possible on the capital invested in the enterprise; social costs and income must also be taken into account. In the long run, it is probably true that private and public economic calculations do as a rule point in the same direction, although cases spring to mind where this is not so.

The authorities responsible for official location policy must be guided by economic calculation. Our knowledge in this field is admittedly limited, and more intensive research and facts, obtained,

---

[1] Since the First World War localities have been officially classified into a number of zones, based on the cost-of-living. The zone classification is reviewed every few years.

e.g., through continuous regional studies, are required. Existing material does, however, already make it possible to indicate some of the main features of a location policy which is rational from the structural point of view.

(1) *Concentration in expanding areas*

The primary task of such a location policy ought to be to encourage the concentration of economic activity in the expanding areas of the country. Within these, in turn, the relatively large concentrations of population are probably those which offer the greatest advantage from the location point of view. At present, official location policy tries to thwart the establishment and expansion of industrial enterprises in our largest population centres, Stockholm, Gothenburg, and Malmö. Firms already established there are encouraged to move to other parts of the country. This is not a policy based on rational economic considerations. These areas, with large and rich markets, and enjoying good communications with the rest of the country and with other countries, are particularly suitable for many kinds of industrial and other activity. This is not to say that firms should be concentrated in the centre of these areas. On the contrary, *within* these regions an attempt should be made to obtain a more even spread between the inner centre and the periphery; but this is first and foremost the job of regional planning bodies. The densely-populated areas are probably the places which management itself frequently has in mind in considering possible new locations and re-location, and there need therefore be no great clash between the private and public point of view.

The official contribution to location policy could then be limited, as it is at present, to giving advice and information and conducting investigations. This must not be interpreted as meaning that the Government ought simply to adopt a passive attitude to location activity and only make its advice and information available when a firm asks for them. On the contrary, the authorities ought themselves to take the initiative in contacting firms and try to ensure, by means of an active information policy, that the public interest in this field is given proper consideration.

Although the Central Government's location policy ought accordingly to be essentially advisory and informative in character, a much greater measure of strict planning and 'direction' may be necessary at the local and regional level in deciding in greater detail where business enterprises are to be located. If the present trend towards the concentration of economic activity in a few densely populated regions continues—and there are many indications that it will—there will be a great need for sensible and flexible town and regional planning. Town planning has long been well developed in Sweden, but despite this deficiencies often occur which hamper the rate of expansion. Local resources in this sector need strengthening. However, it is no longer sufficient that each locality should plan its area independently. In the more densely populated regions economic activity spills over local boundaries, and the small administrative units are becoming more and more interdependent. What is then required is a development survey of the whole area, a regional plan, which describes the geographical conditions of the area, population, economic activity, communications, and the structure of the urban areas, and gives a framework and forecasts for its future growth and development. A plan of this kind is of great value both to the business firms and the authorities interested in location questions. Improved regional planning makes it possible to create areas which are economically viable but which at the same time provide a 'friendly' and settled environment even in densely populated cities. So far regional plans have been drawn up for Stockholm, Gothenburg, and the Borås areas, but more work of this kind is needed in Sweden.

It often proves difficult in practice to get the various units to follow the broad survey plan in their own plans and activity. No body exists with the powers and responsibility for following up the work of planning and co-ordinating action within the subsidiary groups. A solution to this problem is probably to be found not so much in further alterations and extensions in the geographical coverage of local authorities as in a change in the division of labour between local, regional, and central authorities.

(2) *Location problems in areas with employment difficulties*

Most frequently the really difficult location questions arise in areas which are poorly developed economically, where unemployment is abnormally high, and there is a drain on the population. The problem becomes particularly acute if a firm in such an area, perhaps the predominant or sole remaining workplace, closes down. In such cases it is essential for information about any possible cut-back or closing-down of activity to reach the labour market authorities in good time. Experience shows that, if this is done, it has usually been possible to run down the activity or find another solution so that neither the people involved, the local authority, nor the community at large suffered.

The Labour Market Board and the Federation of Swedish Industries have an agreement whereby firms that are planning to curtail or discontinue operations and release labour give two months' advance notice to the Labour Market Administration. In many cases this period is probably too short for the authorities to have time to take the necessary action, and in places where economic activity lacks balance and is weak in other respects a period of notice of about six months is probably more appropriate, and in other places a period of three months. In any case, many firms now give the authorities more than two months' notice of the cessation of operations if they can.

The action to be taken by the authorities on the receipt of such information cannot of course be predetermined in any general way. The natural thing to do in the first instance, however, is to investigate whether the firm's activity can continue on the same scale after some reconstruction and rationalization, possibly involving a changeover to other types of production. It would therefore be valuable if the labour market authorities could make technical and economic knowledge available for such investigations, a service which could possibly be arranged in conjunction with branch[1] or other organizations.

If it proves necessary to wind up the firm, the long-term prospects of carrying on some other kind of production there must be assessed. If none exist, the main contribution of the authorities must be to use labour market policy measures to ensure the area acquires a population structure such that those who do remain there can continue to obtain a reasonable livelihood. In other cases, the most appropriate solution may be for the Labour Market Administration, in collaboration with local authorities and interests, to try to find new enterprises which are willing to establish themselves in the area. Here too information and advice often suffice—vacant industrial premises can be a powerful argument.

Information and advice are frequently not enough to bring about that location which is socially desirable. This may, for example, apply to areas with an unbalanced economic structure or abnormally high unemployment, but which can be considered to have good general prospects of a fuller economic life. From the point of view of the individual firm, however, the area may appear less suitable as a location alternative, perhaps precisely because of the lack of balance or through the poor market prospects to which high unemployment gives rise. Here there is a clash between private and social economic calculation.

Such cases, it is often argued, point to a defect, in that private firms evidently take account of nothing other than the purely commercial cost, whereas they, or at any rate government-owned enterprises, ought to show greater concern. We, however, would go so far as to say that firms—private, central and local government enterprises—ought *only* to take account of the purely commercial factors in their calculations.

[1] See Chapter XIII for a discussion of Branch Councils and Funds.

If the authorities wish to entice enterprises to particular places or regions, they must ensure that those particular areas become so attractive from the commercial point of view that firms go there of their own volition. This can be done through the area acquiring improved general services such as roads, harbours, schools and hospitals. At present local authorities have to meet a large part of the costs of improved services themselves, and this involves an unreasonably heavy burden on an area which is struggling with employment difficulties, or where the economy has stagnated, and it can involve such a high level of local taxation that this discourages location in the area, even if the standard of services has improved. Some adjustment in the allocation of the costs of this activity between the country as a whole and the local area, so that the burden of taxation is more equitably distributed throughout, therefore seems justifiable.

Measures of this type are not always adequate to bring about the establishment of firms on a scale sufficient to solve an area's employment problem. One possibility is to introduce publicly-owned productive enterprises. In so far as the 'excess commercial cost' of location in an area compared with alternative locations could be estimated with any degree of accuracy, the community could accept responsibility for this excess cost during an estimated transitional period, and in this way the area could be made comparable with other locations for private investors. There is a risk, however: firms may be established in this way which have a low profitability from the national point of view.

Moreover, the initial effort must normally be a considerable one if the cumulative effects that are to transform the area from a stagnant to an expansive one are to have a chance to develop. It is probably not enough to lure handicraft or small industries to an area by granting them favours of various kinds. It follows from this that, in the light of the scarce resources of capital which society has at its disposal, the direct control of location must be an exceptional measure.

(3) Recruitment of business by local authorities

It is essential that the 'special actions' discussed above should be directed by the central labour market authorities, since this is the only possible way of obtaining the necessary national perspective for determining which areas, from among all those that wish to boost their local economy, are to be given special Government support. The 'private' enlistment activity which various local authorities conduct in order to attract new enterprise ought to be resisted. Local authorities are usually unable to determine the overall economic consequences of a particular location project, and inducements of subsidies and the offer of other advantages, such as cheap land, loans on favourable terms, or good factory space at subsidized rent, distort the location of industry.

It is often doubtful whether such an acquisition of business really is 'profitable' for a local authority, if the expensive social investment in the form of roads, housing, and drainage is taken into account. It would probably be difficult to exercise greater control over this activity via legislation; instead, the central location authorities must make greater use of information and advisory services to create an understanding of these points on the part both of local authorities and business circles.

(4) *Service problems in sparsely populated areas*

Not every area and region of Sweden can count on obtaining sufficient new enterprise to maintain a flourishing and smoothly functioning community. It would be extremely unfortunate from the point of view of efficiency to dissipate our resources in that way. Some places offer such superior advantages for enterprise that economic activity will increasingly come to be concentrated there. Other areas that are considered capable of long-term development may become desirable locations for new firms through special support measures. A number of areas remain which are not sufficiently attractive in themselves, and for whose benefit the Government ought not, moreover, to adopt any special location measures for the purpose of creating new enterprise. This does not mean that these areas would become completely deserted. On the contrary, many people will remain, and also gain a livelihood in them. On the average, however, they will be very much more sparsely populated than other parts of the country, and they will have great difficulty in building up and financing community services comparable with the level that is normal for the whole country. The Government must then intervene and carry a considerable share of the cost of social services, such as communications, schools, and hospitals.

(5) *The location of Government institutions and enterprises*

So far we have discussed the influence of government on economic activity via general location policy. But the public authorities themselves account for a large part of the economic activity within the country, and of course they have a far greater direct influence over the location of this than in the cases previously discussed. At the same time, the development and location of publicly-owned institutions and enterprises have a strong influence on the location of private economic activity. It is accordingly a matter of great importance that the Government should itself observe principles in the distribution of its

133

own establishments which promote the most rational structure of the economy as a whole. For this purpose it should be possible to follow the broad lines sketched above for location policy in general.

INSTITUTIONAL QUESTIONS

Labour market and location policy must play a central part in an economic policy of expansion. They are not simply supplementary to international trade, credit, and tax policies as means for increasing the mobility of the factors of production; they must also make the necessary adjustments as smooth and painless as possible. Indeed, the capacity of labour market and location policies to find new and profitable employment for the labour and capital which are liberated by this process sets the limits on structural rationalization.

If these limits are not to be drawn too narrowly, the authorities responsible for employment must be provided with far more funds and staff. But the adjustment of the practical content of the policy to current needs will also necessitate the continual exercise of new initiative and independent decision-making, and these will have an impact and significance stretching far beyond the labour market. We do not think it is appropriate to make a Government agency responsible for this, and we consider a special Department for labour market and location questions is necessary. The Department of Industry and Employment recommended in Chapter VI could also, as we have already argued, be entrusted with the work of co-ordinating the activity of the credit institutions and community actions in promoting structural change. Lastly, we think it is only natural that this new Department should also be responsible for the conduct and development of Government-owned enterprises, which are discussed in greater detail in the next Chapter.

PART III
THE STATE AND THE ORGANIZATIONS

CHAPTER XI

THE STATE AND STRUCTURAL CHANGE

The State has been assigned an important place in the co-ordinated economy for which we have drawn up the blueprint in the first two parts. Naturally, the Government is the supreme co-ordinator in the economy, and in our view it must also act as the leader and the prompter in the work of transforming and improving the efficiency of the economy. As the sovereign governing body, the State has of course many other tasks in addition to the purely economic, although the measures it adopts to ensure the rule of law and satisfy social and defence interests and objectives also affect the structure and evolution of the economy. This is not the place to examine and appraise those parts of government activity and their effect on the economy in detail. A general point we do wish to make, however, is that a careful watch should be kept on the long-term structural effects of these measures. Regulations must not be drawn up in such a way that they hamper economic development unnecessarily.

STABILIZATION POLICY AND STRUCTURAL RATIONALIZATION

It is now generally accepted that one of the main tasks of Government is to pursue an active policy for counteracting and mitigating the effects of economic fluctuations. Such action must obviously be short-term in character, since the problem is to eliminate fluctuations in demand and supply which often occur very rapidly, and which therefore necessitate speedy and widely varied measures.

In some cases these efforts to satisfy short-run economic objectives may conflict with attempts to bring about a more rational economic structure. During a general recession, for example, a strong dose of the measures we have already recommended would simply aggravate employment difficulties. This type of situation forces the Government to refrain from some types of intervention in order to avoid the double burden of structural change and anti-cyclical weapons and an excessive strain on employment and individuals.

During a phase of this kind the authorities are under great pressure to find new jobs for redundant workers and to stimulate demand quickly. The danger then of course is that action may be taken to favour the less productive sectors and firms in the economy, where the difficulties appear earliest and are most keenly felt. Labour and capital are then retained in less profitable production, and long-term growth is retarded. It becomes more difficult in addition to maintain short-run equilibrium. In the course of the subsequent upturn the pressure of demand increases, because the rapidly expanding firms have to compete with the stagnating sectors for factors of production. In an incipient inflationary situation of this kind even the less vigorous firms have their survival prospects improved. But when the boom is broken and economic activity begins to decline again, depressionary tendencies are accentuated because the economy contains far too many unproductive firms with inadequate financial reserves.

A disastrous vicious circle of this kind can be broken through deliberate, long-term, and co-ordinated planning of intervention by the Government. Stabilization and structural weapons must be co-ordinated so that they supplement and support, instead of conflicting with, one another. *Vigorous* action to change the structure of the economy should be taken at an early stage of a revival, so that the weaker firms are thinned out and those that have real development prospects can more readily grow and flourish. Measures of this kind also reduce the pressure of demand, and it is easier to resolve the stabilization problem, at the same time as it becomes less necessary to rely on restrictive measures which impede expansion. The international competitiveness of the economy is increased, and periods of recession are therefore likely to be milder, when a smaller proportion of the labour force and capital is tied up in less productive forms of activity.

On the other hand, an active and correct stabilization policy is a prerequisite of successful structural rationalization. The greater mobility and flexibility for which we are striving only appear meaningful if total demand can be maintained at such a high level that the factors of production released from activity which is 'rationalized out of existence' can be absorbed quickly into new and more rational forms of employment.

THE GOVERNMENT MAKES THE RULES

In trying to make the structure of the economy more efficient, the Government must work simultaneously with many different weapons, Broadly speaking, however, it intervenes from two directions. First, it directs the co-ordination of economic policy, and its various administrative decisions determine some of the boundaries or rules to which business firms must pay attention in their own planning and decision-making. Secondly, it participates directly in the life of the economy through its various agencies and enterprises.

As to the outer boundaries, these are not, nor must they become, inviolable rules in the economic game. They must be the subject of continual review, so that they can be adjusted to social and economic changes, and be constructed in such a way that they really do promote the objectives that have been set up. Nor, however, must the principles for government intervention be altered so frequently and arbitrarily that long-term planning by business firms becomes more difficult or even impossible.

Government action should be directed to removing the effects of those sluggish elements in the economy which impede or delay the adjustment of production to new circumstances. But intervention in forms which stimulate movement more directly must also be used if more efficient markets are to be created in which the purchasers are able, through their exercise of choice, to influence the direction of investment and production to a greater extent. Within this framework provided by the Government, the various operating agents, consumers and producers, should have the greatest possible freedom to determine their actions as they see fit. This should tend to increase the 'automatic' character of the economic system and facilitate a rational allocation of resources.

The administrative decisions through which the Government marks out the boundaries for the activities of the interest groups must as far as possible be general in character. But this alone cannot bring about the developments desired. The resistance to change varies between different factors of production, and also for the same factors of production in different economic conditions, or in different geographical areas. General measures must be supplemented with more selective measures, which must be co-ordinated with the general measures and also used with considerable caution, so that they do not grow into an incomprehensible and uncontrollable flora. Above all, care must be taken to ensure that the various forms of Government intervention do not involve subsidizing weak firms and branches, for this would preserve an irrational structure.

THE PUBLIC SECTOR

Since the war the public sector has developed much more rapidly than the private sector, and it now accounts for over one-quarter of domestic economic activity. Within the public sector, the activity of local authorities has shown the most rapid rate of growth, and since the year 1955 its share of public activity has been larger than that of the Central Government. However, the rapid expansion in local authority activity is largely a direct consequence of, or governed by, Central Government decisions, e.g. with regard to education. In other matters the local authorities have greater discretion to carry on an independent policy, and in these instances local authority activity is comparable to the private sector from the point of view of structural policy. In these cases, the co-ordinating Central Government must try to use general and selective methods to influence the activity of local authorities so that they do not obstruct the attempts to create a more efficient economy.

When we speak in what follows about the Government or public sector and its future, we are also including in this expression local authority activity whose scope and direction are in reality determined by central decisions. The more independent activities of local authorities will not, on the other hand, be discussed further in this chapter.

If we begin from the motives underlying the demand by the Government for part of the resources of production, and the way in which the Government obtains payments for the results of its resource uses, this sector can roughly be divided into two categories. The first, the service sector, consists of a number of activities, such as the administration of justice, defence, care of the sick and the elderly, schools, and the greater part of the educational system, which for various reasons it has generally not been considered appropriate or possible to have carried out by private persons or associations. Basic investment activity, such as roads and house building, can also be included in this category, for although commercial arguments have been taken into account when the Government undertook these tasks, these have not as a rule been the decisive arguments. Nor have economic calculations been the sole or most important criteria in considering the scale of these activities, the supply of the 'products', and the determination of price policy.

Secondly, in addition to these services, the Government also carries on commercial activity. Telephonic and postal communications and most railway transport are supplied by Government enterprises, and the Government is the most important entrepreneur in the supply of electric power. Government-owned companies also exist in mining, iron and steel, the forest industries, and a number of other branches. These activities are fundamentally commercial in character. As in the private sector, their planning and their actions are based on commercial calculation.

THE FUTURE OF THE SERVICE SECTOR

In our view a further expansion of the Government service sector is both desirable and inevitable, although it is neither possible nor meaningful to set up any general economic norms for the absolute or relative size of this sector and its rate of growth.

Our argument in favour of a continued growth of the service sector is based on the existence of a strong mutual interdependence between Government service activity and the development of society and the economy in general. Thus the rapid growth of private motoring has necessitated the rapid development of the road network and the replanning of towns. The rising numbers of young and old people, but above all the increased demands for services which accompany a rising standard of living, have necessitated a larger school system and care of the sick and the elderly. Apprentice training, higher education, and research in the natural and social sciences have also had to be extended in order to meet the needs of business firms and satisfy the new demands springing from technical and commercial progress. The trend towards the concentration of economic activity in urban areas and the active labour market policy to stimulate mobility have required more house building. All these are activities of such a character that it is rational and natural nowadays for the community to be responsible for the greater part of them, and this is hardly questioned by anyone apart from a small circle of doctrinaire, old-fashioned liberals.

Despite the great expansion of the Government service sector in recent years, it is still under-developed in many respects. Care of the sick and elderly, education and housing, to mention only a few examples, have still not attained either the quantitative or qualitative standards needed to cope with the demand. In addition to all this, more rapid technical change, expanding markets, population growth, and the general improvement in material standards, will probably mean an increase in the demand for such Government services. This sector must continue to expand rapidly and significantly if the deficiencies in these fields are to be eliminated and we are to obtain a better social balance. If it does not, the expansion of the private sector may become much more difficult or even impossible, and this would bring with it great social problems as well.

THE PRINCIPLES OF GOVERNMENT BUSINESS ACTIVITY

There seems to be broad agreement that the Government ought to carry on a certain amount of business activity where, on grounds of hygiene, social, or practical economic reasons, it appears natural and necessary for the activity to have a marked degree of monopoly. But the Government also conducts enterprises which compete more directly with the private sector of the economy. Here general agreement ceases, and it is often argued that the Government should avoid engaging in such activity.

We consider it is appropriate, and well in line with our general

141

values and objectives, for the Government to own and conduct purely commercial enterprises as well, for rivalry can then develop between them and the private or co-operative enterprises. The outcome of this intensified competition should be more efficient methods of production and distribution, which mean better and cheaper goods for the consumer.

If this competition is to lead to a more rational use of production resources, however, the different groups of enterprises must compete on equal conditions. The Government must therefore refrain from adopting measures which distort competition, either through favouring its own enterprises by special credit facilities, tax reliefs and other commercial advantages or, as generally happens at present, putting them in a worse competitive position by subjecting them to special controls, and requiring them to undertake particular tasks and pay special regard to social policy, defence, or labour policy considerations without giving them adequate compensation.

The reasons for the development of the various socially-owned enterprises have varied markedly from case to case. Non-commercial arguments have usually been prominent, such as emergency requirements, the wish to alleviate the employment situation in a particular sector where a surplus of labour exists, or to avoid the closing down of an enterprise.

In itself this is natural and also defensible. Privately-owned enterprises have a variety of objectives as well, and must take account of social and other matters in their actions. In the case of socially-owned enterprises it is, however, essential to separate the social or other non-commercial costs as far as possible from the purely commercial results. The non-commercial activity ought to be recompensed in a special way by the owner, the community, while the commercial costs should be covered by receipts. This would make it possible to compare the socially-owned commercial enterprises with similar enterprises in the private sector, and judge whether they are rationally conducted and as such justified.

We consider that socially-owned business enterprises ought in principle to be assessed in the same way as firms in other ownership, and be capable of satisfying the same requirements of economic efficiency. If they are to be able to do this, the managers of publicly-owned enterprises must be given sufficient freedom of action so that they can adjust their activity smoothly in the light of rapidly changing conditions. The final right of decision and of power must of course rest with the bodies chosen to represent the owners, the people, but these bodies must limit themselves to dealing with the large questions of principle, drawing up the broad governing lines for the activity and ensuring that the boards of directors they choose follow these directives. Within this broad framework it must then rest with the management proper to accept responsibility for, and arrive at decisions about, the conduct of the enterprises.

CO-ORDINATING PUBLIC ENTERPRISES

At the present time Government business activity presents a very heterogeneous picture, both with regard to the different departments to which the enterprises are responsible and the conduct of their activities. The group consists of enterprises in several widely differing fields of activity, they have a variety of objectives, and are conducted in various legal forms.

The absence of a responsible central management hampers effective collaboration and uniform policy. The first step should be to establish closer collaboration between those enterprises whose activity is naturally related. This may necessitate some formal changes in judicial forms, so that greater uniformity is achieved within the group, and between it and private firms and better conditions are created for flexible commercial behaviour.

Additional co-ordination of Government enterprises requires that in some way or another these should be brought under one unified control. A recent enquiry into Government-owned enterprises[1] suggested that this co-ordination should be brought about within the Administration through placing the enterprises under the Communications Department, which would then resemble a department of industry. This would probably have some advantages from the point of view of the Government enterprise sector, but would on the other hand involve new problems of co-ordination on other matters assigned to different departments. We have already proposed (page 78) that a Department of Industry and Employment should be set up, a proposal which we consider well justified in the light of the growing importance of labour market and location policy. If this department is created it appears natural and appropriate for Government-owned enterprises, or at least a major part of them, to be assigned to it. On the other hand, it seems advisable that those Government enterprises primarily concerned with technical problems of communications should be the responsibility of the Communications Department.

In the private sector co-ordination within the large private and co-operative enterprises is often ensured through special holding companies. This system has proved very beneficial, and it seems it could also be applied to public enterprises. It would mean that these enterprises would be brought together under one or two holding companies, a move for which there may be justification irrespective

[1] *Statliga företagsformer V*, S.O.U. 1960:32. (Forms of State Enterprises V.)

of whether Government business activity is co-ordinated through a particular Government department or not. The arrangement could, it is true, raise problems of co-ordination and allocation of responsibility between the holding company and the Government and Riksdag, but these do not seem to be so insuperable or important compared with the possible advantages of such a scheme from the point of view of efficiency. It would provide an authority with the time, the interest, and the qualifications needed for the successful conduct of a large enterprise. Moreover, this solution has the advantage of providing a clear legal responsibility for the exercise of the duties entrusted to it, since the Companies Act would apply to the holding company and its board.

One of the arguments frequently put forward against this is that the public enterprises have such disparate functions and such few points of contact that there is no practical sense in bringing them all together under one holding company. The reply to this is that all the enterprises need not be placed under one and the same holding company. In addition, if Government business activity does appear very heterogeneous, this is a state of affairs that can be altered by co-ordinating and rationalizing it through a holding company. Finally, there may be advantages from the point of view of the development of the group as a whole in having some dispersion of activity among various types of agency. It reduces the risk of all the enterprises encountering a fall in the demand for their products at the same time, and promotes the stability and long-term planning and development of the group.

The Riksdag must be responsible for determining the duties to be entrusted to a holding company, and only a few of the possibilities will be mentioned here. One of the important duties must be to represent the Government as shareholder at the company meetings of the various enterprises and appoint their boards. It seems probable that the holding company, whose representatives can be assumed to be familiar with the activity of the public enterprises and with management problems in general, will be better able to assess the competence of, and select, the persons appointed to the managerial posts in the subsidiary firms than the bodies which now discharge these duties. Further, the holding company and its board should be able to act as a mediator in negotiations between the various public enterprises on supplies, prices, and so forth.

A holding company would promote greater financial co-ordination and strength, for capital reserves could be accumulated and used for financing the expansion of profitable and growing branches of economic activity without having to use the time-consuming process via the budget discussions of the Riksdag and departments. This co-ordination would also make it easier for the public enterprises to borrow funds in the open market. Finally, the setting up of a holding company would mean that a consolidated account would automatically be obtained for the whole group of enterprises under its jurisdiction.

THE FUTURE OF GOVERNMENT BUSINESS ACTIVITY

It follows from the principles put forward here regarding Government-owned enterprises that, if they are efficiently managed, they will be able to use their surplus income for new investment either within their own enterprises or elsewhere. We take the view that the group has good natural prospects of expanding, and it should accordingly be given the opportunity to exploit them. In such cases new injections of capital would not have to be made in the first instance by the social owners, although these would be provided wherever the proposed projects were economically justified but were too large to be financed by the enterprises out of their own funds. In the same way the public enterprises should be free to raise loans in the market on the same conditions as their private counterparts.

However, there may conceivably be other special circumstances in which the community would be justified in acting as the financier for commercial activity, which would lead to a corresponding expansion of the public enterprise group. In some branches where demand is high there may not be enough competition, production and distribution methods may be irrational, and costs and prices high. It may then be appropriate, for example, to launch public-owned enterprises for the purpose of forcing prices down and bringing about rationalization when other more general methods of increasing competition and reducing costs have proved inadequate.

In other cases, again, the structure of a branch may be irrational because there are far too many small firms competing with one another. If it proves impossible to bring about the desired reorganization in other ways, the Government could intervene here as well and reconstruct the industry by means of direct financial assistance. It has already been pointed out in Chapter X that the Government could provide an impetus in areas where there is unemployment, but which are nevertheless considered suitable for the long-term location of industrial enterprises, by launching publicly-owned enterprises in them.

In practice these last reasons for Government participation in economic activity will probably arise, and be sufficiently powerful to lead to active measures, only in exceptional cases. Changes in the general conditions of business appear instead to be the more important

K

avenue for further direct Government participation in production. The technical and market changes and the need for more fixed capital which we have discussed at various stages suggest that Swedish enterprises, which are comparatively small by international standards and have limited financial resources, will find it difficult to raise the necessary capital to compete successfully with large foreign firms in both the home and world markets. The Government can help here by contributing to, or guaranteeing, the long-term capital needed to carry through capital-intensive projects.

It seems likely, therefore, that the State will need to participate in, and accept the risks of, industrial enterprise on a larger scale in the future. This need not necessarily or solely involve the launching of new public enterprises. But good rapport between the private sector and the Government is essential. The latter can and should collaborate, as financier and leader, with private and co-operative interests, e.g. in the peaceful uses of atomic energy, in market research and marketing in the new and large international markets, in projects for helping the poorer countries to expand, and so on.

The Government can naturally participate in many forms. It may limit itself to accepting some of the non-commercial risks of export sales, or to the provision of credit guarantees for particular projects. But there should also be scope for one or a group of publicly-owned enterprises entering into major commercial projects, either independently or in conjunction with private interests. Whatever form Government participation takes, it must *not* be allowed to lead to the long-term subsidizing of unprofitable economic activity.

CHAPTER XII

THE LABOUR MARKET PARTIES
AND ECONOMIC POLICY

THE RÔLE OF PRIVATE INDUSTRY

The Government is largely responsible for determining the overall governing framework for individual business enterprises through its general economic policy and its own activities as an entrepreneur and provider of various essential services for the citizens. Broadly it could be said that, within this framework, all the individual firm need concern itself with is the best possible commercial results for its own activity. If the framework is 'correct' and if stimulation and compulsion provide adequate impulses, the structural policy tasks of the private sector should then be resolved automatically.

Unfortunately, the matter is not as simple as this. In the first place, the erection of the governing framework is a time-consuming and very complex task, and moreover the requirements for what is regarded as a 'correct' framework gradually change. Secondly, however correct the framework that is devised may be, there are sluggish elements, traditions and liaisons at work in the private sector which delay or distort structural adjustment. The planning and actions of business firms must then satisfy certain requirements if, as is highly desirable, detailed intervention and direction by the authorities are to be avoided.

It is particularly important that business firms should be managed by far-sighted and well-trained managers. The inheritance of business undertakings, and the system in large concerns of having a few individuals serving on many boards of directors, cannot be regarded as satisfactory. It prevents the best powers coming to the top and breeds a narrowness of outlook.

The demands made of enterprises which intend to carry on their activity in the existing type of society can be summarized in the following eight points, in the light of the prospect on the future which we have sketched so far. On each one the community and the trade unions seem to have every justification for providing a stimulus by criticizing and demanding reforms, as well as co-operating with industry:

(1) Business firms must be favourably disposed to internal rationalization and continual technical progress. This may sound trite, but unfortunately it is a requirement that is not always satisfied. All too frequently cost consciousness seems to be lacking, day-to-day

147

rationalization is badly neglected, and the tendencies to rigid prices outweigh the willingness of firms to allow the consumer to share quickly in the profits of rationalization. Administrative and advertising staffs flourish to excess. Competition on service is sometimes carried to such lengths that it results in an unnecessarily broad and expensive structure. Consider the multitude of banks, cheek by jowl, or the network of petrol filling stations. The level of inventories, an expensive item in the production chain, is often managed in far too slapdash a fashion. There are great possibilities for rationalization here which have been neglected so far.

(2) The commercial banks and the trade associations of business firms themselves ought in particular to be more active in their support of structural rationalization. There is no justification for continuing to wait until firms have become bankrupt before intervening in decisive fashion. Structural mergers are better executed when the units that need to be merged, financially or technically, are still sound enterprises. An example of this is the excessively large number of firms in the forest industry. With the trend to larger factories for rationalizing production and the greater need for integration between the supplies of raw materials and the manufacturing end of the industry, the timber and pulp industry would undoubtedly gain in efficiency from having far fewer, but considerably larger, units. The large forest businesses and the banks should try to overcome resistance here, which stems from family traditions and other causes.

(3) At the very least, trade associations should not lend their name directly to the preservation of the existing structure by asking for protection through tariffs or other restrictions and subventions. Since the need for tariff protection is hardly likely to be the same for all the firms in a branch, and the weaker alone cannot be protected, some restraint in these matters from the side of the trade associations would be of the greatest significance. This could also be demanded, but with even greater justification, of such bodies as the Federation of Swedish Industries. Unfortunately, our impression is that these have been and still are far too sympathetic to protection. Thus, unlike LO, the Federation of Industries and the Export Association have not explicitly expressed support for *lower* tariffs. The same contrast exists in particular sectors, e.g. between the Textile Industries Federation on the one hand and the Textile Workers' Union on the other. It would be extremely helpful if business organizations were also willing in practice to work for a stronger economy, not simply by rationalization *within* each firm and branch, but also through improving the prospects for the most productive and profitable branches of industry.

(4) The medium-size and small firms of the engineering industry in

particular will face growing problems as a result of the increasing need for market research, more expensive selling and service costs, and credit facilities in export markets. The merger is sometimes a solution to this problem, although in many cases it may not achieve much because the products may be quite different. Collaboration in other forms, such as market research and the provision of service facilities in foreign markets through joint repair workshops and offices, can, however, be rewarding.

(5) An extremely large part of the economy consists of small enterprises, which have an important place to fill as sub-contractors or purveyors of local services. But it is essential that the small firms should be well conducted and managed so that they can enjoy the economies of both large- and small-scale production. This necessitates greater specialization between firms on the production side, and the setting up of joint sales organizations, something that is particularly important in export sales. The initiative in bringing this about ought to rest in the first instance with the trade associations in handicrafts and industry, but there should be fruitful co-operation in this field between them and the State. Small businessmen themselves must show a real willingness to tackle the problems of structural policy.

(6) There is frequently a waste of specialists and other personnel in short supply through firms competing recklessly with one another and with the Government for their services. Scarce resources of personnel could sometimes undoubtedly be used more effectively through the joint conduct of research and experiments, and through setting up jointly-owned research institutes and laboratories from which firms could order the jobs they wish to have carried out, instead of undertaking the work independently themselves.

(7) The private sector must learn to know more about itself, and provide very much more information to outsiders, to its employees, and to the public. This can be done by providing more resources for such institutions as The Industrial Council for Social and Economic Studies,[1] which can promote much needed self-examination and provide a stimulus to new methods. In line with this there is sociological and other research touching on the environment of the workplace, the problems of the employees, indeed the whole range of questions concerning human beings in the production process. Firms must collaborate with educational organizations and with the Labour Market Board, and devote more resources to staff training and further training in every type of job and grade.

[1] This organization (Studieförbundet Närlingsliv och Samhälle, or SNS) was formed in 1948 by businessmen and social scientists to promote the study of social and economic questions by private business.

(8) The place of the employee in the firm enters into both the last-mentioned areas. Suggestions activity,[1] and collaboration between management and the workers on methods, organization, and job satisfaction, must be intensified; it is only through the employees knowing why and how changes in production and methods take place, and through their having some influence on them, that they can acquire an interest in and make an appropriate contribution to production.

Almost all of the above points may seem self-evident, and hardly worth mentioning. But however obvious they may seem, they are so far from being generally satisfied that it seemed necessary to emphasize them in this analysis. In each one of them there are naturally strong trade union interests at work; the trade union movement, as one of the parties to production, must endeavour to ensure that they are given concrete content. These demands regarding the private sector's own contribution to structural policy may therefore well come to be included in future collective bargaining.

THE RÔLE OF THE UNIONS

We have already developed the point that one of the main tasks of Government economic policy is to remove the obstacles to, and create inducements for, increased adaptability on the part of the factors of production. Not only labour market policy, but tax, credit, international trade, and anti-monopoly policies have been regarded from this point of view. The main idea has been that greater adaptability allocates the factors of production in a manner favourable to economic expansion.

The primary objectives of trade union policy differ from that set out above. Its main objectives can briefly be said to be the following:

(a) the creation of a 'rational' wage structure, i.e. a structure in which the wage differentials between different groups and individuals are determined by the nature of the input of effort, and

(b) ensuring a reasonable share of the national product to wage earners as a whole. Two additional, but secondary, objectives can also be distinguished;

(c) trade union policy ought to be conducted in such a way that it does *not* prejudice economic equilibrium;

(d) moreover, at least it ought *not* to obstruct the structural shifts in the economy which are the prerequisite of expansion. The negative

---

[1] An agreement of 1946 between LO and the Swedish Employers' Confederation on the subject of Works Councils contains provisions governing suggestions put forward to employers by their employees.

formulation points to the secondary character of these last two objectives. Here we are only concerned with (*d*), which refers to the structural aspect.

In general, it can be said that trade union policy in Sweden has been moulded in a way which does not work counter to the continual adjustments of the economy to new technical factors and changed market conditions. There is much less use in Sweden than in many other countries of training and recruitment barriers, conditions for entry to, or transfer between, trade union organizations; in brief, restrictive practices are practically unknown. The principle of industrial unionism, which with few exceptions is now the prevailing one, is undoubtedly the form of trade union organization which best facilitates a successive and smooth adjustment to changes in production. Traditional demarcations according to work processes or jobs, which are common in countries where the trade union movement adheres strictly to the craft principle, have proved an obstacle to rationalization. Unhampered movement between organizations within a sector of the economy and the right to transfer freely between unions that organize wage earners in different sectors are in fact extremely important conditions for enabling technical progress to lead to rapid increases in productivity.

Nor can the wage forms and wage systems applied in Sweden be said to hamper productivity. Nowadays payment-by-results in various forms accounts for over 60 per cent of the total wage bill in industry, and the trend is upwards. Wages are adjusted to technical changes through continual revision of piece-work prices, an important task for local trade union branches and factory clubs. On the other hand, the trade union movement in Sweden is opposed in principle to profit-sharing systems. It is highly questionable whether such systems can have any very obviously favourable effects on productivity. Finally, the differences that used to exist as a result of different (or in many cases no) pension schemes, which hampered mobility in various ways, have been removed through the introduction of the National Pension Scheme.

THE WAGE POLICY OF SOLIDARITY

Although it can thus be said that neither the forms of trade union organization nor the wage system as such conflict with the general economic policy objective of promoting adaptability and expansion, there may, on the other hand, be some doubt about whether this objective is reconcilable with the goals of wage policy and with the forms for its execution. Two wage policy principles conflict here.

One is that accepted by the trade union movement, namely a wage policy based on solidarity between groups, the object of which is to create a rational wages structure. The opposite point of view, which has found support especially among businessmen, can be most simply denoted as 'the capacity to pay principle'. The capacity to pay of enterprises and branches ought to be the decisive element in wage setting, and consequently relative wages ought to be an expression of differences in the profitability of enterprises rather than of differences in the nature of work. The question we should try to answer is which of these principles best promotes the objectives of flexibility and rapid growth?

At first sight the capacity to pay principle seems preferable to the solidarity principle from the points of view that are relevant here. It can be argued that a system of wage determination in which the wages of the profitable firms are higher than those of the weak and contracting firms and branches of the economy ought to facilitate the transfer of labour from areas of surplus to areas of shortage, and thus be an active factor in structural change. However, the argument is based on an assumption which is by no means incontestible, namely that moderate wage differentials provide a sufficiently strong inducement to labour mobility. Both Swedish and foreign investigations raise strong doubts about the correctness of this assumption. The wage is simply one factor among many which determine the recruitment and mobility of labour, and in all probability wage differentials would have to be very wide for the desired effect on mobility to be achieved. In practice, the probable consequence of wage differentials is that weak enterprises can often exist thanks to a 'wage subsidy' from underpaid workers. Thus the effect in many cases is to preserve firms that are not profitable in the long run rather than to promote the exodus of labour to high wage enterprises.

But even if the model were to function according to the assumptions, i.e. if labour were very mobile in response to wage changes, objections could be raised, although from a slightly different starting-point. A collective agreement whose structure was based entirely on capacity to pay would be subject to rapid cyclical fluctuations; it would also give rise to continual demands for the restoration of differentials and become an active factor in the inflationary mechanism.

In its most extreme and systematic form, the wage policy of solidarity may appear to preserve the structure of employment, since it deliberately refrains from attempting to use wage differentials as inducements to move. This ignores the fact that the continual pressure from the side of wages which wage solidarity is assumed to exercise on the weaker enterprises must compel firms to rationalize and, when these possibilities have been exhausted, to close down. This is probably a more effective way of bringing about the transfer of labour to more productive enterprises than the creation of wage differentials, on the assumption of course that there is a high level of employment in the economy and that an active labour market policy is pursued which uses re-training, grants and other measures to mitigate local difficulties of adjustment which the wage policy of solidarity accentuates, even if it does not create them.

The experience of recent years has indicated that the scope for a wage policy of solidarity which helps to change the structure of the economy has hitherto been rather limited. Solidarity has had its greatest successes when its aspirations have coincided with market tendencies. It succeeded, for example, in raising the wages of agricultural and forestry workers during and immediately after the war, when there was a scarcity of foodstuffs and forest products. On the other hand, attempts during the past few years to adjust the wages of typical low wage industries towards the average for industry as a whole have not given satisfactory results. Market forces have, primarily through wage drift, modified those wage differentials created through collective bargaining which were an expression of the wage policy of solidarity. From this the conclusion could be drawn that, where the economic position of sectors with poor wages is very weak, the trade union movement cannot make any very fundamental contribution to the elimination of wage differentials without the support of a much better and more efficient labour market policy than that which has been applied hitherto.

It should be clear from what has been said that the wages policy of solidarity, in conjunction with an effective labour market policy, operates strongly to promote the efficiency and expansion of the economy. It remains to discuss briefly whether this view has to be modified in the light of the co-ordinated forms in which wage policy has been conducted in recent years. It is a common misconception that co-ordinated wage rounds are by nature schematic and rigid, that they do not, in the same way as the traditional wage round at union level, provide scope for the expression of the special wishes of particular groups, which may be justified and conditioned by lagging, by technical conditions, or other circumstances. Historically, there may be some justification for such a view. The first central wage agreements were either linked to index numbers or made use of general figures for wage increases that were binding on every group. Subsequently, however, it has been possible to incorporate in the co-ordinated wage agreements greater elements of differentiation, and the structure which they now have no longer makes it possible to argue that they are part of a rigid and irrational system of wage fixing. LO's Wage Policy Council[1] now functions as a preparatory body, helping the secretariat to draw up the guiding lines for some differentiation within the framework of a centralized wage policy. This also allows scope for direct negotiation at union level with the union's counterpart, whereby the distribution of the wage increases *within* the area covered by a union allows further differentiation. Finally, there are local negotiations about the application of the agreement, and these fall to the local trade union organizations. Thus a good deal of care is taken to ensure that collective bargaining policy in its currently strongly centralized forms does not bind the wages structure too rigidly in an irrational and restrictive way.

However, wage policy is no longer the sole task of a mature, strong trade union movement such as that in Sweden. Trade union activity reaches out into ever larger areas of the life of the community. Indeed, the active co-operation of the trade union movement is essential to the successful pursuit of an economic policy of the kind we have sketched here. The Swedish trade union movement has long been positive in its attitude towards problems of efficiency, at the level of the firm, the branch, and society. The high level of employment which has prevailed for a long time has meant that the process of rationalization has not been felt as a threat to the security of the individual to nearly the same extent as it was in earlier periods, and that it has generally been possible to master difficulties of adjustment. Organizational strength, peaceful conditions on the labour market, intensive trade union education activity, these are some of the factors which have almost certainly contributed to a realistic awareness on the part of the union members of the relationship between economic efficiency and the standard of living. Finally, enduring collaboration between the trade union movement and the political wing of the labour movement in the Government has meant that the Swedish trade union movement has paid far more attention to, and to some extent felt responsible for, economic tasks than the unions in many other countries.

At the level of the individual firm this attitude has, for example, found expression in the activity of works councils, which in part deal with questions of productivity, while the local trade union organizations are already involved when a firm is faced with problems of adjustment. These problems are likely to arise on a much larger scale in future, and we accordingly envisage that the unions and their branches will have to shoulder new burdens. They ought in our view to play an active part in the transfer of labour, the induction of new

[1] This is an internal group which L.O. set up shortly after the discussion of wage policy at its congress in 1951. The Council now consists of seven members (a majority) of the L.O. executive secretariat.

employees, re-training, training and other questions which are likely to arise in connection with the greatly increased labour mobility which may be one of the results, and in part is one of the objectives, of the economic policy we are recommending.

Trade unions and the central trade union authorities can also make a significant contribution to a more productivity-conscious economic policy. The trade union movement has tremendous opportunities for influencing developments in the desired direction through the opinions it expresses and the attitudes it adopts on various issues. More attention should be paid in trade union education and information work to questions of economic structure. Finally, the unions can, either independently or in conjunction with other organizations, conduct research into the problems of adjustment for the human factor of production that arise from greater mobility in the economy. More attention should be paid in the trade union movement to sociological research of this kind.

CHAPTER XIII

CO-ORDINATING BODIES FOR STRUCTURAL RATIONALIZATION

BRANCH COUNCILS AND BRANCH FUNDS

While the Government must be responsible for creating the framework for the pursuit of economic efficiency, and management must have the direct responsibility for realizing these ambitions, there is considerable scope here, in our view, for collaboration and co-ordination between the parties on the labour market. The idea of co-operation at the level of the individual industry or branch is an old one, and originates mainly in the efforts of the labour movement to create industrial democracy alongside political democracy. Thus the idea of branch councils appears in the 1923 enquiry into the problems of industrial democracy, and it recurs in the Post-war Programme of Swedish Labour, which suggests agreements between the trade unions and employers with a view to securing greater influence for the workers in planning within each branch. Several of the post-war Government enquiries into particular industries have proposed setting up permanent organs, whose main job would be to conduct investigations, give advice, and put forward suggestions. Committees of this kind have, however, only been formed in the shoe and textile industries, and only the two sides of industry, but not the community or the consumer, are represented on them. In 1947 LO proposed to the Government that a permanent body should be created for the purpose of co-ordinating the work of investigation and planning relating to the rationalization and development needs of industry and trade. But the proposal was strongly resisted by the Federation of Industries, and was dropped.

Two main arguments can be clearly distinguished in discussion about the idea of branch councils. The original and more important was the attempt to give employees some influence in dealing with the common problems of a branch; the second, and in later discussion the more prominent reason was entirely economic, namely that joint discussions between representatives of management and employees were regarded as one possible way of increasing efficiency within the branch. There is a clear connection between these two reasons, in that economic democracy can in itself be a stimulus to rationalization, but our interest centres essentially on the efficiency aspect of the branch council idea. The question we ought to raise and attempt to answer is then as follows: can we expect organized co-operation between management and employees in different branches to make a positive contribution to promoting expansion in these branches? If the answer is in the affirmative, we ought then to ask what forms such co-operation can appropriately take. Very little guidance in answering these questions can be obtained from the organizations for co-operation which have already been created, both because they are so few and because they have been operating for such a comparatively short period, during which they have not had time to develop any noteworthy activities.

If the question is restricted to the purely economic significance of branch councils of the type discussed hitherto, we are inclined to assess this as fairly limited. In Sweden it has been assumed that they would be formed voluntarily and not, as for example, in Norway, through legislation, and that they would only be advisory. Nor has there been any discussion of their obtaining financial resources over and above what may be needed to carry on some investigation work. Thus councils of this type cannot work actively for structural rationalization by purchasing weak enterprises or by giving credit to growing enterprises. Under these conditions their activity must be limited to questions of a more general character and to recommendations to the member firms. It is quite possible for them to take the initiative in a number of valuable matters such as training, research, statistics and market investigations, and they can in this way serve a positive purpose in the continuous process of rationalization. But it is difficult to see how branch organizations of this kind could become instruments of an active policy of structural rationalization, which in practice must of course involve mergers into stronger business units, support to the expanding parts and firms in a branch, and the acceptance of decline, losses and liquidation for others. Co-operation at branch level, with or without consultation with representatives of the employees, always runs the risk of being bedevilled by a preoccupation with maintaining a structure in which the weaker enterprises also retain their position. There is also a considerable risk that a common branch front may be presented to outsiders, and this can very readily acquire a touch of protectionism.

These risks could in some measure be reduced through a broader representation in the branch councils; if both the public and the consumer interests were represented the councils would have a broader outlook, and selfish tendencies within the groups would be restrained. On the other hand, the work might then lose its drive, and both discussions and action might be kept at an even more general level than would be the case if the parties in the branch alone carried on discussions with one another.

Thus we do not think it likely that an enlarged system of branch councils with the tasks and resources they have had so far can be a really significant factor in the process of expansion which we regard as desirable, irrespective of whether they are representative only of the two sides of industry or of a larger number of parties. This is not to say, of course, that the formation of branch councils may not be desirable on grounds other than those discussed here, e.g. for promoting an understanding of conditions in different branches. We have therefore endeavoured to find other forms of branch co-operation which could better satisfy the objectives formulated above. An essential requirement for this to happen is in our view that branch organs should be allocated funds which can be used for structural rationalization purposes.

The simplest form for this could perhaps be a levy on the wage costs (e.g. the research levy in the building industry) or total turnover of the branch. But such an arrangement would probably require legislation, which we are unwilling to recommend in the first instance. The other alternative which we consider is worth experimenting with is the creation, through the machinery of collective bargaining, of *branch rationalization funds*. The main justification for this idea is the one stated earlier, namely that of discovering ways in which business firms can co-operate in backing the forces of expansion. But at the same time we are seeking a form which satisfies another objective which has been discussed earlier. Economic expansion must be based on more capital formation, but in a form which does not involve a continual increase in the concentration of property among the owners of capital.[1] For this reason we have already rejected a general increase in self-financing by business firms as the essential basis for economic growth. Branch rationalization funds would make it possible to combine the desire for capital formation without concentration of property to particular individuals *and* the need for an active structural policy conducted at branch level.

These branch rationalization funds could be constructed along the following lines. Funds would not be established through legislation, fixed dues, or binding agreements of any kind, but would instead be built into the general collective bargaining system normally applied by the parties in the Swedish labour market. Wages and conditions of work would of course continue to be the main objects for negotiation. But when, as at present, there is increasing agreement in principle about the need for more capital formation in order to promote a more rapid rate of growth, but no agreement about the most suit-

[1] Since this report was written the Minister of Finance has appointed an official committee to investigate the structure of ownership and concentration of power in business.

able form for this, it seems reasonable to solve this distribution question in the same way as others, namely through free bargaining. Alongside the ordinary wage negotiations, the parties could bargain about allocations to branch funds, to be used for increasing the efficiency of the branch. To begin with, when the assets of the funds were limited, resources could be spent on research, market investigations, consultation activity of various kinds, experiments in special forms of occupational training, and so on. As the supply of capital increased, the funds could be used for more ambitious economic projects, such as the financing of expanding firms, temporary support to firms which were considered to have good long-term prospects, or the liquidation of unprofitable enterprises.

Objections can of course be raised to the basic assumption underlying this idea, namely that both parties are sufficiently interested for such negotiations to take place. Only practical experience can of course show whether the system is workable. We think it is worth a trial just because we consider that this basic condition is satisfied. In traditional wage negotiations, what are the practical alternatives to allocations to a branch fund? For the employer the main alternative is a rise in wages which extracts funds from the firm and from the branch. For the wage earners the situation is more complicated. The wage policy of solidarity often puts the workers in strong firms and branches in the position where they are forced to refrain from a wage increase that would otherwise be possible. The money remains instead in the enterprises. This leads to a growth in the assets of the owners of capital, even if at the same time it consolidates the enterprise and improves its competitive position. Both sides should then have a greater interest in making allocations to such funds; entrepreneurs in retaining profits for the branch, wage earners in avoiding the consequences of the wage policy of solidarity for the concentration of assets, and at the same time strengthening the expansionary forces of the branch. But there are of course also strong restraining forces at work on both sides. The entrepreneurs are interested in safeguarding the prospects of the individual firm, the employees in driving up the take-home pay. The equilibrium point for these tendencies, which are partly in harmony and partly in conflict, can only be determined by bargaining. In any event, the flexible collective bargaining system which has been developed and proved through the years in Sweden is the essential basis for our proposal being put into effect.

Another possible objection is the fear of group egoism which has been mentioned in connection with the branch council idea. This is probably more justifiable regarding branch councils than the branch funds discussed here. In the case of the latter, the main task is assumed to be that of making productive use of the resources collected by the branch itself. This alternative provides no real scope for selfish branch behaviour; on the contrary, the branch funds can be expected to harmonize with more general wishes regarding structural policy.

If the fear persisted that the creation of the funds could lead to unwarranted favouritism towards the special interests of the branch, this could be prevented in various ways. In the first place, the view LO expressed earlier about the representation of several parties in branch councils should apply with even greater force to branch funds. Thus both the public and the consumer should be represented on the boards of the funds. The Government could appoint the chairman of the board and the consumer organizations could have the right to appoint some of the members. It would be only reasonable to allow the majority, and thus the power of decision over the use of resources, to rest with the representatives of the parties subscribing the funds. Another measure to prevent the branch from becoming completely self-centred would be to allow some part of the funds to go to a central fund which had more general objects than those of the branch funds.

Finally, the setting up of branch rationalization funds might arouse disquiet of a more ideological, social and philosophical kind. This device undoubtedly means that the growth of capital in society would correspondingly take place in institutes without owners, in foundations with a somewhat diffuse principal. To our way of thinking this is a merit rather than a defect. The idea has been developed to some extent by Ernst Wigforss,[1] who sees in 'social enterprises without owners' an alternative to Government and privately-owned enterprises. But while Wigforss seeks successively to undermine the private right of ownership in existing enterprises—and does not indicate in any concrete way how the process is to take place—our idea broadly involves the retention of the right of ownership to existing enterprises, but a gradual harnessing of the required increase in capital through 'foundations without owners'. A trend towards enterprises without any formal physical owners has in fact been occurring in various forms for a long time in the economy, with a view to preserving the great economic power of the interests of private capital when the right of ownership is curtailed by tax legislation. It occurs through holding companies, through firms obtaining large direct interests in one another and, finally, through the formation of tax-free foundations. The last two forms are particularly interesting, because the directors are self perpetua-

---

[1] See, for example, his *Kan dödläget brytas?* (Can The Deadlock Be Broken?) Stockholm, 1959.

160

ting. Institutions of the 'foundations without owners' type also exist in the National Pension Funds, where representatives of the workers, employers, and the public interest administer large funds without any clearly definable directions and on their own responsibility. In this fundamental matter of principle, our proposal therefore involves nothing new; what is new is that the branch funds would be set up through negotiations, not via legislation. This would also make it possible to devise more flexible rules governing the use of the funds.

It is clear, and quite in line with our view of social development, that economic growth in a highly industrialized, democratic, welfare society ought to take place in different forms from those of the past, and that the private sector—by which is meant the method of financing rather than the apparatus of production—should become successively less important as the foundation of economic progress. The progress we make and are determined to make in the future is not simply the result of the contributions by the owners of capital, but of our joint efforts. Since we do not believe that either general socialization or sharply increased taxation should form the main lines of advance for attaining our general economic policy objectives, we are prepared to accept the consequences for the structure of ownership, namely the growth of a new sector to which in the long run our proposals must lead, which we term *social enterprises without owners*. It is not for us to develop the ideas about greater industrial democracy.[1] Our main concern is the productivity aspect; but we consider that our productivity-geared proposal can readily be combined with the points of view that can be put forward on the basis of a desire to extend industrial democracy at the branch level.

It was pointed out in the introduction to this section that at this stage we propose to limit ourselves to a sketch of branch rationalization funds, and so it is not necessary to discuss the precise details. It would be valuable if practical experience could be obtained from some sectors where a palpable need for collaboration between the parties had already led to the formation of co-operative bodies. If one or more of these bodies could be extended in the way that we have indicated the strength of our argument could be tested. We are also anxious to point out that we are not trying to advise against branch co-operation in the form of branch councils where no financial participation through fund building occurs. But we have formed the view that branch councils of the type discussed earlier have fairly limited possibilities, and that attempts should not be made, either through legislation or central agreement, to bring into being

---

[1] This was the subject of another report presented to, and debated at, the 1961 L.O. Congress: *Fackföreningsrörelsen och företagsdemokratin* (Trade Unions and Industrial Democracy), L.O., 1961.

institutions that have little chance of functioning effectively. Finally, we consider that the voluntary approach to the formation of branch funds should be tested first before consideration is given to legislation for prescribing dues or allocations to rationalization funds with similar duties.

THE NATIONAL PENSION FUNDS

In the last section we discussed appropriate forms for co-operation between businessmen and wage earners and representatives of the public interest and of consumers, for the purpose of promoting more capital formation without private or Government ownership and for channelling these streams of capital into productive uses. In this connection we are by no means unaware that an institution which to some extent fulfils these requirements already exists in the National Pension Funds. However, it seemed more appropriate to discuss this question in general terms first, for two reasons. The National Pension Funds, through their link with the retirement pension system, have a special legal position and are governed by a special Act, and in addition the existing regulations for the administration of the funds impose such strict limitations on the types of investment in which their resources may be placed that the funds can hardly operate at present as an instrument of an active rationalization policy.

The first circumstance is mainly formal in character. The retirement pension scheme is a pure re-allocation system, and thus funding is not an integral part of the insurance system, apart from the small fund necessary as a buffer between contributions and benefits. This has been justified on economic grounds, and the task of the fund has been said to be mainly that of countering the decline in saving which it was considered would follow from the introduction of the pension system, and also of contributing more generally to an increase in capital formation. But if the allocation principle has once been abandoned through funding, there is nothing to prevent the general objective of increasing capital formation through this fund from being given a more prominent place. If one is convinced that total savings in society are insufficient to satisfy generally accepted investment needs, an increase in saving through funding may be a reasonable long-term solution. It would account for part of the capital formation which in the last resort should provide the real basis for higher material standards, of which improved pensions are in turn a part. Thus we consider that the size of contributions to the pension fund ought to be determined by reference to the fact that it must be one of the means for creating long-term equilibrium between savings and investment requirements.

As the National Pension Funds become increasingly important

162

for the total capital formation in society—it can be anticipated that by 1970 the funds will account for between a quarter and a third of total net savings—the second of the special circumstances named above, the narrow restrictions on investment, comes into prominence. The rules require the resources of the funds to be placed only in debentures and in local authority bonds. In theory, these rules could be maintained until the point was reached where the growth in the funds corresponded to the capital requirements of the public sector and of housing production, and to that part of the private sector's requirements which takes the form, or is permitted to take the form, of bonds, i.e. at present essentially a small part of the financial requirements of the financially strong industries. If small-scale industry, handicrafts, commerce and other parts of private industry form their own credit institutions, this sector can be extended even under the current investment rules for the funds. Even with this extension of the bond market, a saturation point for investment outlets can, however, be anticipated. Quite apart from this, it scarcely seems desirable to divide the capital market into two sectors, the National Pension Funds being directed entirely towards the bond market (with a natural emphasis on central and local government borrowing) while other savings are placed in mortgages, bonds, and in other ways. Other institutions besides the National Pension Funds, particularly the insurance companies, will need to find an outlet in bonds and, as has already been said, the bond market cannot be expanded above a certain limit. Further, the yield on a pure bond portfolio can be expected to be less than that from a more widespread lending policy. It is of course desirable that the resources of the Pension Funds should be administered so as to give the maximum yield. But even more important is the fact that this sort of division would condemn the Pension Funds to the passive administration of their resources. With a sufficiently large accumulation of funds, supported by a tight fiscal policy, the shortage of capital can eventually be expected to ease, and there will then be greater scope for a more active lending policy on the part of the private credit institutions. Our thesis is of course that during periods of credit rationing lending follows well-worn paths, which are determined, at least in part, by relations with former bank customers and similar considerations.

We are quite unwilling to regard the investments which the funds now make and, if the existing investment rules are retained, will be directed to undertake in the future, as less productive than those of the insurance companies and commercial banks. On the contrary, since they consist mainly of basic investments in housing, roads, schools, and hospitals, they are quite indispensable for the development of our economy and welfare society. On the other hand, there

163

are limits to the possibilities of the funds being able to exercise a decisive influence on the structure of the economy through providing credit for such investments and in the forms bond lending involves. The division of the capital market which we see emerging in the future, between private credit institutions that can determine the main features of the direction of economic activity through their lending policy, and the National Pension Funds, which have passively to ensure that the level of social services is adjusted accordingly, should be prevented. We consider that it should be possible for the National Pension Funds to become the instruments of a more active structural policy, an objective that can only be achieved through some modification of the rules governing their investments.

It is not for us to indicate in detail the ways in which this should be done. At one point, on the other hand, the lending provisions of the funds are at present too 'generous'; we refer to the re-borrowing rules, which have not, it is true, been used on any scale so far, but which are irreconcilable with the desire for a freely functioning capital market. They ought to be repealed at once. Finally, modification of the investment rules for the funds does not mean that we are aiming at giving them a privileged position, but solely at their being placed on an equal footing with other credit institutions. Obviously, the administration of the funds ought also to be subject to the same supervision by the monetary authorities as other credit institutions. This should be done through having the Riksbank represented on the boards of Pension Funds.

CO-ORDINATION BY CONSENT

The general and selective methods of government economic policy form the framework within which both public and private enterprises and institutions have to operate. It is the Government that must mark out the broad lines of advance and determine the balance between private and public needs and the size of the public enterprise and service sectors. We envisage that on this basis the proposed Department of Industry and Employment should then be responsible for directing the work of co-ordination in the economy. It should draw up a flexible general plan for the structural developments in the economy which are considered most advantageous and desirable, on a *purely economic assessment* of trends at home and abroad. This general plan should then be used as a basis for discussions with representatives of business, industry, the labour and credit markets with a view to finding a common line of advance.

We wish to make it clear that this co-ordinating work is not intended to be a method whereby the Government tries to persuade industry to accept social or other obligations that are not commercially justified, but simply a way of trying to co-ordinate structural evolution on economic grounds. If the Government wishes industry to accept non-commercial obligations these must be made the subject of special agreement, and business firms must be compensated for any extra costs that arise in the process.

This general plan does not involve detailed planning, but is a method of indicating certain broad lines of development for the expanding and profitable sectors and branches. Planning of this kind faces the major difficulty of assessing the prospects for different branches of production at a time when the price mechanism is becoming an increasingly unreliable indicator of real alternative costs because of international and domestic distortions of prices and through the divergence between social and private costs. This means that the compilation of even the most general plan for the economy must be based on extensive calculations and forecasts, to which current and future prices are incomplete guides.

In Chapter VI we recommended the establishment of a Department of Industry and Employment under the charge of a cabinet minister. This department should be responsible in the first instance for labour market questions and questions concerning private industry which are not covered by particular departments (e.g. agriculture and communications), and for most public enterprises. Since the department would have to undertake extensive research as a basis for co-ordination, it would need to have a competent research department at its disposal. The fruits of this work would then be used by the department to draw up the general plan, after consulting representatives of industry. The means of achieving the objective set up would then be discussed with those departments, chiefly the Ministries of Finance and of Trade, which are responsible for economic and international trade policy, with the credit institutions, Pension Funds, public enterprises holding company, Government-owned bank and, finally, with the labour market authorities and organizations. Investment questions would, as we proposed in Chapter VI, be discussed in the first instance by a broadly representative investment council.

The essential point about planning of this kind is that the object of the discussions must not be for the Government to dictate to industry, but to ascertain in what ways economic policy can best be co-ordinated with the actions of private industry and the labour market organizations in order to provide for a more rapid rate of economic expansion and higher productivity, from which every group gains.

In view of the harmony that must exist among the various groups with regard to the structural evolution of industry itself, co-ordination based on discussion and agreement is very much preferable to a more formal procedure. The parties are then prepared to accept their share of responsibility for events, something that can never be imposed upon them, measures can be adjusted more readily to suit changing circumstances, a mutual trust is established and contact with opinion maintained which make it easier to solve the problems that arise in future, and so on. On the other hand, the possible results that can be achieved are naturally limited by what the parties consider, or can be persuaded, is in their own interests.

Against the background of the broad framework set by the State, and the results that can be achieved through discussion and mutual exchanges, the various organizations and institutions can then evolve their own policies.

SUMMARY

The general background to this programme is the challenge which the Swedish economy will have to face from new technologies and the associated requirements of more capital and increased adaptability, the integration of international trade policy in Europe, the industrialization of the under-developed countries, and the competition regarding economic expansion between the democracies and communist states.

Our aim has been to fit Swedish structural policy into this framework, on the basis of certain generally accepted values of the working class movement—freedom, democracy, security, greater equality, free choice for consumers, an improved social balance, and international solidarity. Our objective, which follows from these values, is rapid economic expansion, in order to create the material basis for greater freedom and security, increase our prospects for helping the under-developed countries, and vindicate democracy in the current race between political systems. This objective can be made somewhat more precise in the following requirements: full employment; the use of the resources of production in accordance with the wishes of the consumers, but also in the light of the need for social balance; greater equality, both between various groups within the country and between the rich and poor countries; a structure of production and a social and working environment which take fuller account of the needs, happiness and adjustment of those engaged in productive life.

In our view, the attainment of these objectives necessitates greater geographical, functional, and temporal and technological mobility or adaptability on the part of the factors of production. This can be achieved through removing various obstacles such as trade barriers, agreements in restraint of trade, formal requirements of competence on the part of labour, and through measures designed to stimulate adaptability directly, such as increased international competition and better re-training facilities.

Free competition and planning are often contrasted with one another as pure systems of economic policy. We have not based our programme on either, but have instead begun quite empirically from the mixed economy characteristic of the present structure of our economy. This mixed economy is regarded as both the most likely and the most appropriate system for the period this programme can reasonably be considered to cover.

In an economy of the present type we cannot expect competition to become so wide in scope that it alone could determine the course

167

of development. Even if, against all the odds, this were to prove possible we would not regard it as a fortunate solution. Many major needs cannot be satisfied through the typical profit economy; much intervention and redistribution are necessary. At the same time, competition can *to some extent, within the framework* of certain Government controls and intervention and, in particular, through free trade, be *one* of the measures at work in an economic policy directed to bringing about structural adjustment.

A completely planned economy which satisfied our requirement of free choice by consumers would encounter many grave problems. It would be susceptible to political pressures and the stresses that can arise when great expectations and practicable results cannot be reconciled. At the same time, the size of the public sector and the need for various forms of social intervention in the economy mean that a large measure of official direction is inevitable. This should be as well planned and co-ordinated as possible.

In addition to competition and the various forms of social intervention which also aim at promoting competition, various associations and organizations operate to balance one another as centres of countervailing power. Their interests differ so much that they provide a mechanism which almost certainly operates more fluently than competition. The structural policy followed by society must, as we see it, make use of all these three means, and our programme attempts to co-ordinate them.

Part I contains an introductory account of our general starting-point, values, objectives and general framework. Part II examines the Policy Framework which the authorities have to pursue with regard to credit, tax, and international trade policy, the supervision of competition and prices, and labour market and location policy. Part III discusses the rôle of the State in providing services and acting as an entrepreneur in its own right, and the rôle of the private interest groups, i.e. the structural tasks of private industry and the place of the trade union movement.

A more active *labour market and location policy* provides the foundation on which the remaining measures build. In this process, two conditions must be satisfied; first, full employment must be maintained and, second, labour mobility must not lead to social and economic difficulties for the private individual. The stimulus of more attractive opportunities, greater freedom for the individual worker and salaried employee to select and change his job, place of work, and place of residence, will encourage a more rapid change in structure which harmonizes well with social requirements.

But this labour market and location policy must accept more explicitly the need for change and movement, and operate in step with the trend towards greater concentration of business enterprise and of population. Its main objective must not be to conserve business enterprises and communities, and it must overcome the opposition to urban areas, and in particular to large cities. Further, it must be given the opportunity to supplement the purely commercial assessments of location areas by business enterprises—the sole assessment which businesses *should* make—by social and economic considerations, in close consultation with private industry. Given an active and more aggressive labour market policy, it will be possible and appropriate to use international trade, tax, and credit policy to provide greater compulsion and greater stimulus to adaptability within the economy. We therefore propose very definite changes in all three areas.

International trade policy must be more consciously directed towards liberalization and the easing of restrictions. The protectionist features which still characterize our trading policy, and have even been intensified in recent years, must be eliminated. Long-standing customs barriers can no longer be justified by reference to general employment arguments.

Credit policy must very largely be viewed against the background of a strong fiscal policy. Fiscal policy must contribute to bringing about economic equilibrium, to restricting the demand for capital, and reducing the problems of priorities in credit policy. This is particularly important since a shortage of capital in relation to the existing propensity to invest is likely to persist in the foreseeable future. Indeed, this is probably inevitable under full employment. The liberalization of the credit market must therefore in all circumstances be relative, and preferential treatment will be demanded for the housing market and for public borrowing unless fiscal policy is sufficiently strong. But, apart from this, liberalization should be the aim. The price which it may be necessary to pay for this in the form of a more flexible interest rate policy can be accepted without any evil social consequences, in the light of the existing distribution of claims and assets among various social groups. Further, liberalization must be supplemented in other ways by more planned social measures to increase the free flow of capital. The large capital requirements for new investment—atomic power and branch rationalization—will necessitate increased collaboration by the Government via the budget, the Pension Funds, the public enterprise sector, and so on.

Tax policy can be regarded as an extension of credit policy and as the basis of fiscal policy. Tax controls must be tightened up and made administratively easier, the taxation of physical persons must be reconstructed to avoid unnecessary tax irritants and to make a sufficiently large total tax yield politically possible. This will probably necessitate some reduction of progressiveness in the lower and medium income brackets, and in return increased indirect taxation. However, we are very doubtful about the wisdom of relying to any great extent on higher indirect taxation in the form of a turnover tax, and we accordingly recommend that other alternatives should be considered. A reconstruction of the costs of social insurance ought probably to be given priority here, so that they are financed more through employer contributions, along the lines of the National Pension System. In the case of company taxation, we recommend a changeover in whole or in part from the existing taxation of net profits to taxation on the basis of gross expenditure, primarily because the taxation of net profits helps to preserve the structure of enterprises through the particular reliefs it provides for less expansive and less profitable enterprises.

The framework policy also includes the *promotion of greater competition, general supervision of prices,* and *more consumer guidance* as essential features of the search for greater adaptability. One of our recommendations is that the burden of proof with regard to the injurious effects of restrictive practices ought to be reversed. It should not be necessary for the public to have to prove that a particular restriction on competition is harmful. Business firms should be under an obligation to prove that it is not injurious in the light of cartel legislation.

Part III discusses the place of the State and of the organizations. Our first demand here is for more systematic, long-term and coordinated planning of government intervention; stabilization policy measures must be fitted into the general perspective of structural policy in quite a different way from past practice. This applies both to the determination by the State of the 'framework' and 'the rules of the game', and to the Government's own activity as an entrepreneur and as the provider, together with the local authorities, of the public service and basic sector. *Government business enterprises* also stand as much in need of changes in organization as any other sector, and we propose one or more holding companies, and a change of direction, so that internal structural adjustments and expansion, transfers to new activity, and a more active investment policy become possible within the public enterprise sector. This will enable it to compete on equal terms with private and co-operative firms and concerns. The service sector must be continually strengthened in order to bring about social balance, and the conditions created for ensuring the continued growth of the public sector in step with the demands for higher standards and for more education, social policy, and a more active cultural policy.

With regard to *private business* we have, while fully recognizing the useful contributions it has made and is making, considered we are entitled to demand even more active policies both by individual enterprises and the more 'co-ordinating' organs, such as the commercial banks and the organizations in particular branches. A more positive outlook by business to international trade liberalization and to mergers and integration of business firms would be particularly encouraging.

Finally, *the place of the trade union movement* is discussed. More rapid changes in structure, and in particular the intensification of labour market and location policy, will make it increasingly possible for the trade unions to pursue an active wage policy, not least in the typical low wage sectors. Less attention will need to be paid to preserving employment in less profitable firms when better jobs can be offered in more expanding firms, and the scope and operational area of wage policy will therefore be extended. It should be possible to exercise additional pressure from the side of wage policy, and this in turn will not only increase the possibility of a wage policy of solidarity but also make a major contribution to the promotion of an efficient economic structure.

However, the rôle of the trade union movement is not confined to wage policy. It has traditionally had a positive outlook towards any economic policy which increased efficiency, and it has had a stimulating effect both through the Confederation and the national unions, and at the local level, e.g. through works councils. We assume that the unions will face additional tasks in this area. In our view, they ought to play an active part in the transfer of labour, in the initiation of new workers, in training, and in influencing the surroundings of work. At a more central level, we assume that the branch funds we have recommended and more centralized wage negotiations will give the unions greater scope for exercising pressure on, but also collaborating with industry and the authorities in, the process of structural change.

Our programme concludes with proposals for certain institutional changes, covering a large number of possibilities—a more active use of National Pension Funds, the setting up of branch funds and branch councils, the organization of public enterprises, the establishment of a Department of Industry and Employment, the formation of an investment council, and better co-ordination of international trade policy. These are expressions of the increased co-ordination we recommend for a structural policy which is based on definite values and objectives, which aims at more rapid and flexible adjustment and mobility, but which, precisely because of the emphasis on adaptability, does not assume that any detailed blue-prints of the economy of the future can be drawn up in advance.

171

INDEX

173

INDEX

Government Borrowing, *see* Credit
Policy
Growth, rate of, 37

Housing, finance, 58, 60, 70–1; and
mobility of labour, 123–4
Höglund, R., 76n

Industrial Council for Social and
Economic Studies, 149
Industrial Democracy, 156, 161
Industrialization, 18
Import Controls, 22, 96
Institute of Economic Research: and
savings, 61; and interest rates, 72
International Trade, 24, 25, 26, 92;
policy, 58, 92; and division of labour,
92; European integration, 99–101;
economic co-operation, 25; economic policy, 106–8; labour market
policy, 104, 107; trade unions, 105–6.
See also Protection, and Under-
developed Countries
Investment, private, 38, 61–2, 68, 71;
public, 34; ratios, 68–70; levy, 90;
reserves, 85, 89
Investment Council, 79, 165

Labour Market Administration, 77,
119, 130, 131
Labour Market Board, 78, 107, 119,
123, 127, 130, 149
Labour Market Policy, 59; and adaptability, 41, 124–5; forms, 119–20;
international trade, 104, 106–7; job
induction, 125; and placement,
120–1; loans, 78. *See also* Adaptability, and Mobility
LO, and branch organizations, 156,
160; labour market policy, 119;
price controls, 113–14; tariff policy,
105, 107. *See also* Trade Unions
Location Policy, 59; current, 126–8;
and aims, 128–9; areas of unemployment, 130–2; control of, 129, 132;
government institutions and enterprises, 133–4, 145; private and public costs, 128, 131, 132, 142; service
problems, 132–3. *See also* Local
Authorities, and Planning
Local Authorities, 67, 127, 139–40;
recruitment of firms, 132–3

174

Minister of Trade, 113, 115
Ministries: Finance, 165; Trade, 165
Mobility, 41; functional, 42; geographical, 42, 120, 121, 122; occupational, 120, 125–6; stimuli, 121–3;
wage differentials, 46, 153–4; handicapped workers, 126. *See also*
Adaptability, Housing, Labour Market Policy
Monopolies, *see* Restrictive Practices

NATO, 25
National Pension Funds, 53, 63, 71,
79, 84, 151, 161; and capital formation, 162–3; investment rules, 163–4

OECD and OEEC, 27, 101

Planned Economy, 51
Planning, regional and town, 128, 129,
130. *See also* Economic Plan
Population, 18
Price Controls, 113, 115; committee
on, 113, 116; LO and, 113–14
Price and Cartel Board, 110, 111, 114,
115, 116, 117
Prices, rigidity of, 44, 45, 111, 113;
flexibility, 115; recommended, 114;
supervision, 114, 115; unreasonable,
114. *See also* Restrictive Practices
Private industry and structural policy,
147–50
Private sector, future, 161
Production Council for Industry, 128
Profitability, 38
Protection, and balance of payments,
98–9; employment, 96–7; infant industries, 97; structural aspects, 107;
terms of trade, 99; under-developed
countries, 104; war, 99. *See also*
Dumping, and International Trade
Public Enterprises, 132, 133–4, 140–6;
co-ordination, 143–5; costs, 142;
holding companies, 143–5; management, 142–3
Public Sector, 22, 34, 139–40; and
planning, 52; consumption and investment, 68–70

Rationalization, 35, 36, 76, 145, 148,
157
Research, 24, 149, 155; market, 51

For Product Safety Concerns and Information please contact our EU
representative GPSR@taylorandfrancis.com
Taylor & Francis Verlag GmbH, Kaufingerstraße 24, 80331 München, Germany